Carnegie Mellon University

Pittsburgh, Pennsylvania

Written by Dan Liebermann

Edited by Christina Koshzow, and Jon Skindzier

Layout by Kimberly Moore

Additional contributions by Omid Gohari, Christina Koshzow, Chris Mason, Joey Rahimi, and Luke Skurman

ISBN # 1-4294-0036-9
ISSN # 1551-9686
© Copyright 2006 College Prowler
All Rights Reserved
Printed in the U.S.A.
www.collegeprowler.com

Last updated 5/16/06

Special Thanks To: Babs Carryer, Andy Hannah, LaunchCyte, Tim O'Brien, Bob Sehlinger, Thomas Emerson, Andrew Skurman, Barbara Skurman, Bert Mann, Dave Lehman, Daniel Fayock, Chris Babyak, The Donald H. Jones Center for Entrepreneurship, Terry Slease, Jerry McGinnis, Bill Ecenberger, Idie McGinty, Kyle Russell, Jacque Zaremba, Larry Winderbaum, Roland Allen, Jon Reider, Team Evankovich, Lauren Varacalli, Abu Noaman, Mark Exler, Daniel Steinmeyer, Jared Cohon, Gabriela Oates, David Koegler, Glen Meakem, and the Carnegie Mellon University Bounce-Back Team.

College Prowler®
5001 Baum Blvd.
Suite 750
Pittsburgh, PA 15213

Phone: 1-800-290-2682
Fax: 1-800-772-4972
E-Mail: info@collegeprowler.com
Web Site: www.collegeprowler.com

How this all started...

When I was trying to find the perfect college, I used every resource that was available to me. I went online to visit school websites; I talked with my high school guidance counselor; I read book after book; I hired a private counselor. Sure, this was all very helpful, but nothing really told me what life was like at the schools I cared about. These sources weren't giving me enough information to be totally confident in my decision.

In all my research, there were only two ways to get the information I wanted.

The first was to physically visit the campuses and see if things were really how the brochures described them, but this was quite expensive and not always feasible. The second involved a missing ingredient: the students. Actually talking to a few students at those schools gave me a taste of the information that I needed so badly. The problem was that I wanted more but didn't have access to enough people.

In the end, I weighed my options and decided on a school that felt right and had a great academic reputation, but truth be told, the choice was still very much a crapshoot. I had done as much research as any other student, but was I 100 percent positive that I had picked the school of my dreams?

Absolutely not.

My dream in creating *College Prowler* was to build a resource that people can use with confidence. My own college search experience taught me the importance of gaining true insider insight; that's why the majority of this guide is composed of quotes from actual students. After all, shouldn't you hear about a school from the people who know it best?

I hope you enjoy reading this book as much as I've enjoyed putting it together. Tell me what you think when you get a chance. I'd love to hear your college selection stories.

Luke Skurman
CEO and Co-Founder
lukeskurman@collegeprowler.com

Welcome to College Prowler®

During the writing of College Prowler's guidebooks, we felt it was critical that the information within was unbiased, and that the guides were unaffiliated with any college or university. We think it's important that our readers get honest information and a realistic impression of the student opinions on any campus—that's why if any aspect of a particular school is terrible, we (unlike a campus brochure) intend to publish that fact. While we do keep an eye out for the occasional extremist—the cheerleader or the cynic—we take pride in letting the students tell it like it is. We strive to create a book that's as representative as possible of each particular campus. Our books cover both the good and the bad, and whether the survey responses point to recurring trends or a variation in opinion, these sentiments are directly and proportionally expressed through our guides.

College Prowler guidebooks are in the hands of students throughout the entire process of their creation. Because you can't make student-written guides without the students, we have students at each campus who help write, randomly survey their peers, edit, layout, and perform accuracy checks on every book that we publish. From the very beginning, student writers gather the most up-to-date stats, facts, and inside information on their colleges. They fill each section with student quotes and summarize the findings in editorial reviews. In addition, each school receives a collection of letter grades (A through F) that reflect student opinion and help to represent contentment, prominence, or satisfaction for each of our 20 specific categories. Just as in grade school, the higher the mark the more content, more prominent, or more satisfied the students are with the particular category.

Once a book is written, additional students serve as editors and check for accuracy even more extensively. Our bounce-back team—a group of randomly selected students who have no involvement with the project—are asked to read over the material in order to help ensure that the book accurately expresses every aspect of the university and its students. This same process is applied to the 200-plus schools College Prowler currently covers. Each book is the result of endless student contributions, hundreds of pages of research and writing, and countless hours of hard work. All of this has led to the creation of a student information network that stretches across the nation to every school that we cover. It's no easy accomplishment, but it's the reason that our guides are such a great resource.

When reading our books and looking at our grades, keep in mind that every college is different and that the students who make up each school are not uniform—as a result, it is important to assess schools on a case-by-case basis. Because it's impossible to summarize an entire school with a single number or description, each book provides a dialogue, not a decision, that's made up of 20 different topics and hundreds of student quotes. In the end, we hope that this guide will serve as a valuable tool in your college selection process. Enjoy!

OMID GOHARI ◯ CHRISTINA KOSHZOW ◯ CHRIS MASON ◯ JOEY RAHIMI ◯ LUKE SKURMAN ◯
The College Prowler Team

Table of Contents

Introduction from the Author

When people ask me where I'm going to college, I'll sheepishly reply, "Carnegie Mellon University." It's with a look of sheer stupefaction that they nod approvingly, having never heard of the school and thinking me a fool for receiving my college education from a grocer. On the other hand, the people I talk to who are aware of the University's incredible accomplishments respond differently. Their faces light up and they energetically reply, "Really? Wow, you must be smart!" The way things are going, I might be hearing this reply much more often.

Carnegie Mellon University is growing and improving so rapidly that its name recognition hasn't caught up with it yet. It's only in the last twenty years that the University has begun its ascent into the upper echelon of the nation's colleges, a place where it is sure to stay for some time. If one thing is happening on campus, it's growth. As the University expands its size and academic options, the school's students continue to grow with it. Carnegie Mellon is intent on molding its students into professionals, and it succeeds.

Honestly, I'd never even heard of Carnegie Mellon until it was time for my college search. It's hard to paint an accurate portrait of the school with just facts and statistics. CMU has a unique cultural dynamic that defines the University in the eyes of its students. When you have a professional University, composed of five nationally-commended colleges in fields ranging from computer science to the fine arts, you're guaranteed a certain level of intellectualism. When you have students from around the world participating in a campus environment where diversity is embraced and treasured, all wrapped in the hills of Pittsburgh, Pennsylvania, you're guaranteed a certain level of perspective. Some students would even say that when you have a Carnegie Mellon degree, you're guaranteed a certain level of salary.

If you're interested in CMU, you probably already know all that it can offer you in terms of academics and professionalism. Now be prepared to ask yourself a larger question. Do you want to spend the next four years of your life there? No matter how much information you know about a college, that's not an easy question to answer. Hopefully, this book can provide you with some insight into what life is really like at Carnegie Mellon University.

Daniel Lieberman, Author
Carnegie Mellon University

By the Numbers

General Information

Carnegie Mellon University
5000 Forbes Avenue
Pittsburgh, PA 15213

Control:
Private

Academic Calendar:
Semester

Religious Affiliation:
None

Founded:
1900

Web Site:
www.cmu.edu

Main Phone:
(412) 268-2000

Admissions Phone:
(412) 268-2082

Student Body

**Full-Time
Undergraduates:**
5,258

**Part-Time
Undergraduates:**
271

**Total Male
Undergraduates:**
3,351

**Total Female
Undergraduates:**
2,178

Admissions

Overall Acceptance Rate:
42%

Early Decision Acceptance Rate:
53%

Regular Acceptance Rate:
41%

Total Applicants:
14,114

Total Acceptances:
5,869

Freshman Enrollment:
1,367

Yield (% of admitted students who actually enroll):
23%

Early Decision Available?
Yes

Early Action Available?
No

Early Decision Deadline:
November 1

Early Decision Notification:
December 15

Regular Decision Deadline:
January 1

Regular Decision Notification:
April 15

Must-Reply-By Date:
May 1

Applicants Placed on Waiting List:
2,709

Applicants Accepted from Waiting List:
271

Students Enrolled from Waiting List:
120

Transfer Applications Received:
309

Transfer Applications Accepted:
45

Transfer Students Enrolled:
30

Common Application Accepted?
Yes

Supplemental Forms?
Yes

Admissions E-Mail:
admissions.office@cmu.edu

Admissions Web Site:
www.cmu.edu/enrollment/admission

SAT I or ACT Required?
Either

SAT I Range (25th–75th Percentile):
1290–1480

**SAT I Verbal Range
(25th–75th Percentile):**
610–710

**SAT I Math Range
(25th–75th Percentile):**
680–770

Retention Rate:
94%

**Top 10% of
High School Class:**
69%

Application Fee:
$60

SAT II Requirements For:

**Carnegie Institute
of Technology and
Architecture:**
Math I, Ic, or IIc, Physics or
Chemistry, Writing

**Humanities and
Social Sciences:**
Math I, Ic, or IIc, Writing, plus
one additional test selected
by applicant

**Mellon College of Science
Computer Science and
Industrial Administration:**
Math I, Ic, or IIc, Physics,
Chemistry, or Biology, Writing

Information Systems:
Math I, Ic, or IIc, Writing, plus
one additional test selected
by applicant

Financial Information

Tuition:
$32,044 per year, plus a $40
registration fee per semester

Room and Board:
$8,606

Books and Supplies:
$910 per year

**Students Who Applied For
Financial Aid:**
60%

**Students Who Received
Financial Aid:**
52%

**Average Need-Based
Financial Aid Package
(including loans,
work-study, grants,
and other sources):**
$21,658 per year

**Financial Aid Forms
Deadline:**
February 15

Financial Aid Phone:
(412) 268-8186

Financial Aid E-mail:
thehub@andrew.cmu.edu

Financial Aid Web Site:
www.cmu.edu/hub

Academics

The Lowdown On...
Academics

Degrees Awarded:
Bachelor
Master
Post-Master's Certificate
Doctorate

Most Popular Majors:
12% Computer Science
11% Business Administration
10% Computer Engineering
 7% Mechanical Engineering
 6% Information Science

Undergraduate Schools:
Carnegie Institute of Technology
College of Fine Arts
College of Humanities and Social Sciences
Mellon College of Science
School of Computer Science
Tepper School of Business

➡

Full-Time Faculty:
806

Average Course Load:
5 courses

Faculty with Terminal Degree:
98%

Graduation Rates:
Four-Year: 66%

Five-Year: 78%

Six-Year: 81%

Student-to-Faculty Ratio:
10:1

AP Score Requirement
Possible credit for scores of 4 or 5

IB Score Requirement
Possible credit for scores of 6 or 7

Special Degree Options
Dual-Degree Programs: Biomedical Engineering, Engineering and Public Policy, Biology and Psychology

Accelerated Master's Programs: Public Management and Policy, Information Systems, Business Administration

Intercollege Programs: Bachelor of Humanities and Arts, Bachelor of Science and Arts, Science and Humanities Scholar

Sample Academic Clubs
The Law Society, the National Society of Black Engineers, the Investment Club, the Society of Hispanic Professional Engineers, the Filmmaking Club

Best Places to Study
Library, University Center

Did You Know?

"The two universities that have made the **most phenomenal gains** [in the last two decades] are Stanford and Carnegie Mellon."
–George Keller, author of *Academic Strategy: The Managment Revolution in Higher Education*

Want to go to class without leaving your dorm? Carnegie Mellon now offers a **few of its courses online**.

Need help on your test? Just go inside the front door of Baker Hall. Students in the School of Humanities and Social Sciences often **rub the nose of Hamerschlag's statue** for good luck.

Once a semester during finals, students gather outside during the middle of the night to participate in Primal Scream—a chance to yell, eat food, and relieve stress.

Carnegie Mellon assigns **"unit" values instead of "credits"** to each of its courses in order to represent the amount of work that is required by a particular class. One unit equals one hour of work, so a nine-unit class means that you'll have approximately nine hours of work a week. Most classes are between nine and twelve units.

Students Speak Out On...
Academics

"Academics are excellent! The personal attention you get from your professors, who are the best in their fields, is unbelievable."

Q "**The teachers in the art department are good**. I really respect them. Some of the others have gotten lazy, and they're more interested in research than in teaching classes."

Q "The teachers at CMU are very nice. They are always willing to lend a helping hand, and the teaching assistants (TAs) are usually pretty good. **There are always a few who slip by and end up teaching a subject they have no experience with**, but the majority of TAs are extremely well-qualified. Some have even taught the course in previous semesters."

Q "It really depends on the subject and the teacher on a case-by-case basis. Overall, the professors are very dedicated, but some teachers are just straight morons and it's impossible to figure out why they teach. **My physics professor didn't know the first thing about educating anyone on the subject**, and I swear my English professor was a raving drunk who just pulled the entire class discussion out of his butt every Tuesday and Thursday. On the other hand, I've learned invaluable things from some very professional teachers on the subjects of video, design, and anthropology."

Q "Usually, dealing with administrative stuff is extremely frustrating, but the academic experience is great if you have the right professors. There will always be a few professors you'll hate, but the ones that you really grow to enjoy **make it worthwhile**."

Q "Professors tend to be better as you get older. Unfortunately, there are a lot of teaching assistants and lower-level professors who speak in strong accents and make things difficult. I've found that **the level of knowledge is phenomenal**, but lots of professors are more interested in research than in students. It really depends on the professor."

Q "This school is excellent, academically. It is ranked in the top 25 universities in the country. It's the best place in the world to study robotics. It ranks in the top 10 for engineering, computer science, and business. Plus, the College of Fine Arts has numerous famous alumni. In fact, the school of drama is in the top three of all theater programs in the United States and is also the oldest drama degree-granting program. **The teachers are easily accessible**; they all have office hours, and most of the classes are pretty small, so you can ask questions."

Q "Teachers and academics are awesome! If you come here, **you'd better be serious about learning**, because you will get swept away if you aren't. Pretty much everything we do here is good. All of our sciences kick butt, and our drama and theater programs are really exceptional, too. We are cool like that; we have both nerds and artists. It makes things interesting."

Q "The quality of education **depends on your major**, I guess. From the few classes I've taken in H&SS (Humanities and Social Sciences), I think the University's humanities department isn't that great—at least, the introductory courses aren't. If you're into a technological field, then the school is not bad. The computer science program is not bad at all. The teachers usually know what they're talking about, unlike most other places. Regardless, it really depends on your major."

Q "The professors are pretty good here; it depends on the class. I got to know my business professor really well. He knew all of our names (there were 85 of us) within the first few weeks, and we see him everywhere. He always stops and chats for a little while. He's also the head of the business department. If you make an effort, **you can really get to know your professors**, but as far as teaching quality goes, I guess most professors are good. Everyone has his or her own favorites. The teachers are great at what they do and are into cutting-edge research, so they're never out of touch with what is modern. You can't be ranked as high as CMU is without having good professors."

The College Prowler Take On...
Academics

It often feels like CMU is just a school with brilliant students struggling to get by in a never-ending onslaught of hard work. In the rush of our academic diligence, CMU students can often forget the role our professors play in furthering our education. That said, CMU professors run the gamut from "I'm a pioneer in my field" to "I'm teaching this class so I can do research here." One thing that can be said about all the professors, though, is that they're very approachable. Professors will always find time to meet with you after class or respond to your e-mails. As a student, your relationship with your professors is largely what you make it.

The University's excellent academic reputation is the reason why most prospective students become interested in Carnegie Mellon in the first place. The school maintains an interesting dichotomy with its success in both technological and artistic pursuits. Many people consider CMU's technical majors to be the most successful, and accordingly, they've received national acclaim. In the academic stratosphere, computer science and engineering reign high above most other majors. The sciences, business administration, drama, and information systems programs are also held in high esteem while the humanities maintain a nebulous space at the bottom of the school's academic spectrum.

A-

The College Prowler® Grade on
Academics: A-

A high Academics grade generally indicates that Professors are knowledgeable, accessible, and genuinely interested in their students' welfare. Other determining factors include class size, how well professors communicate, and whether or not classes are engaging.

Local Atmosphere

The Lowdown On...
Local Atmosphere

Region:
Northeast

City, State:
Pittsburgh, Pennsylvania

Setting:
Medium-sized city

Distance from Cleveland:
2.5 hours

Points of Interest:
The Andy Warhol Museum
Carnegie Museum of Art
Heinz Field
Heinz Hall
Kennywood Park
The Mattress Factory
Oakland
PNC Park
Point State Park (The Point)
Schenley Park
Shadyside (Walnut Street)
South Side (Carson Street)
Squirrel Hill (Murray Avenue)
The Waterfront

→

Closest Movie Theaters:

Cinemagic Manor Theatre
1729 Murray Ave.
Squirrel Hill
(412) 422-7729

Cinemagic Theatre
5824 Forward Ave.
Squirrel Hill
(412) 421-7900
Loews at the Waterfront
300 W. Waterfront Dr.
Homestead
(412) 462-6384

Closest Shopping Malls:

The Waterfront
Monroeville Mall
Ross Park Mall

Major Sports Teams:

Penguins (hockey)
Pirates (baseball)
Steelers (football)

City Web Sites

www.city.pittsburgh.pa.us

http://pittsburgh.citysearch.com

www.wpxi.com/pittsburgh

Did You Know?

5 Fun Facts about Pittsburgh:

- In addition to being called **one of America's most livable cities**, Pittsburgh is also known as the City of Champions, thanks to its legendary sports teams.

- **Pittsburgh is a beer town**. Home to a number of breweries, the city makes its local favorite, Iron City, right here.

- *The Mothman Prophecies*, *Dogma*, *Silence of the Lambs*, *The Wonder Boys*, *Kingpin*, *Night of the Living Dead*, *Inspector Gadget*, and **many more movies were filmed here**.

- If you like **nice stadiums**, **Pittsburgh has two of them**. Both the Pittsburgh Pirates and the Steelers have two state-of-the-art facilities on the North Shore.

- **The Duquesne Incline** and the Monongahela Incline are cable cars that run up the side of Mt. Washington and provide riders with a fantastic view of the city.

Famous Pittsburghers:

Christina Aguilera

George Benson

Rachel Carson

Perry Como

Stephen Foster

Jeff Goldblum

Ahmad Jamal

Michael Keaton

Gene Kelly

Henry Mancini

Dennis Miller

Mr. Rogers

Gertrude Stein

Andy Warhol

August Wilson

Local Slang:

Pop – what a Pittsburgher calls soda

Yinz/yunz – rumored to have originated from "you ones;" similar meaning as "y'all"

Gumband – rubber band

Red up – to clean up

Students Speak Out On...
Local Atmosphere

"There are tons of museums around campus, if you're into that kind of stuff. My favorite place to go on the weekends is the Waterfront. They've got shopping, great restaurants, and a huge movie theater."

Q "I don't feel like I've seen much of Pittsburgh. **It's so spread-out**. I heard the Strip District is nice."

Q "Although CMU is in the city of Pittsburgh, I'd say that it's on the outskirts of the city and closer to a few suburbs. We're down the street from Pitt, but since our school is on a campus and not along several streets, it's rare that you see Pitt kids up here. **Stay away from the drunken frat boys** during your freshmen week of orientation—they can get pretty rowdy, especially if you walk around with everyone from your whole dorm floor!"

Q "**Pittsburgh is not an exciting town**. It's a strange mix between a suburban mini-mall atmosphere and a major national city with tons of residential areas mixed up in-between. Yeah, there are tons of other universities present—Pitt, Chatham, Duquesne, Point Park, Robert Morris—but chances are, if you are at CMU, you won't have any desire to socialize with these people anyway. Most likely, you'd prefer a quiet evening of staying in your dorm room and gaming online with your friends. Go to a Pirates game, because the stadium is sweet beyond words."

Q "There are lots of good theaters downtown and on campus. We've got one of the best drama programs in the world, so take advantage of that as much as possible. **The baseball park is nice, too, and tickets are cheap**."

Q "One thing that sucks is that **stuff tends to close really early around here**. I don't get it at all, but it's true. Besides that, we have the Steelers, the Penguins, and the Pirates not even 10 minutes away by car. Museums, downtown, and Kennywood's roller coasters are all really close. You can always find something cool to do."

Q "I like Pittsburgh. It's a nice medium-sized city. I think **it's beautiful because of the mountains and rivers**, and I find enough to do here. We have some really great museums just down the street. If you like sports, there are the Steelers and the Pirates. The symphony is excellent, and there are some good theaters, although the best place for theater is on campus—the school of drama does around 15 different shows a semester. We also have a big park adjoining our campus. With the University of Pittsburgh, Duquesne University, Chatham College, Carlow College, Robert Morris College, and some community colleges all nearby, the city is quite student-friendly."

Q "You're in the good old city of Pittsburgh. It's a good town to go to school in because you can get your work done without having to worry about seeing all of the marvelous things there are to see. Besides partying and clubbing at semi-decent nightclubs, there are some nice museums, sporting events, and shows you can catch, but it's nothing like a major metropolitan city. I'd **stay away from the Hill District**, though."

Q "The University of Pittsburgh is just down the street. There are bars and clubs down there. The **guys and girls are more attractive at Pitt**, but not many places are open really late. Clubs and bars close around 2 a.m., unless they're after-hours clubs."

The College Prowler Take On...
Local Atmosphere

Allegheny County may be one of the most elderly counties in the nation, but that doesn't make Pittsburgh any less of a college town. With Pitt right down the street and Duquesne and Chatham nearby, lots of local stores are tailored to college crowds. If you like coffeeshops, there's more than enough of them in the area surrounding CMU to satisfy your thirst. During the school year, you can't go wrong walking down Forbes or Fifth Avenue—chances are you'll stumble upon some concert, restaurant, party, or bar. In addition, the residential neighborhoods of Squirrel Hill and Shadyside are a nice complement to Oakland's college atmosphere. These nearby areas offer students some variety in upscale dining and shopping. For the adventurous student, downtown Pittsburgh has a lot to offer as long as you know where you're going. Unfortunately, however, Downtown does not offer the same youth and cultural scene as larger cities like New York or Chicago.

There are always activities going on in the area, ranging from sporting events to plays, rock concerts to symphonies, and raucous clubs to romantic dining. Despite the large quantity of events happening nearby, many students are disappointed to find out just how small of a city Pittsburgh actually is. Begin to explore the area slowly. The amount of entertainment in Pittsburgh is limited, and trying to run through it all will leave you without any resources for the future.

B-

The College Prowler® Grade on

Local
Atmosphere: B-

A high Local Atmosphere grade indicates that the area surrounding campus is safe and scenic. Other factors include nearby attractions, proximity to other schools, and the town's attitude toward students.

Safety & Security

The Lowdown On...
Safety & Security

Number of CMU Police:
17

CMU Police Phone:
412 268-2323 (emergencies)
412 268-6232
(non-emergencies)

Safety Services:
Campus Watch
Emergency Phones
(RAD) Rape Defense classes
Safe Walk
Shuttle/Escort Van

Health Services:
Basic medical services
Counseling and
psychological services
On-site pharmaceuticals
STD screening

Health Center Hours:
Monday, Tuesday, and
Thursday 8 a.m.–7 p.m.,
Wednesday 10 a.m.–7 p.m.,
Friday 8 a.m.–5 p.m.,
Saturday 11 a.m.–3 p.m.

Students Speak Out On...
Safety & Security

"In my opinion, CMU's campus is really safe. We'll occasionally have conflicts, but as long as you use common sense and don't walk down a shady avenue at two in the morning, you'll be fine."

Q "**I feel pretty safe on campus**, even walking around late at night. There are blue call boxes around campus, just in case there is an emergency. Supposedly, you can see one from everywhere on campus, but I don't know if anyone has actually tested this. This past year, I lived off campus and used the CMU escort service several times. It's a van that picks you up on campus at several locations and then drops you off at your residence. It's pretty convenient, and great for leaving a friend's dorm, the library, or maybe even the [computer] cluster late at night."

Q "The campus has had its share of assaults—sexual or otherwise—but they are few and far between. **CMU is in a city with plenty of dark alleys to walk down**, so you have to exercise caution and judgment, but if you act somewhat appropriate, you should be safe. The police try very hard to make the socially naïve student body feel comfortable in Pittsburgh. Just don't walk around in certain areas by yourself later at night. It's always a good idea to go places with friends, and if it's nighttime, and you're going someplace you're unfamiliar with, take the bus."

Q "The campus is relatively safe. The biggest problem, I think, is bike theft. Not much happens on campus other than **drunken kids being rowdy**. There is a crime report section on the CMU Web site, so you can check that out."

Q "The crime rate has been very low; most crimes involve **stealing bikes and unattended laptop computers** or underage drinking on campus."

Q "I think that **things are pretty safe** on CMU's campus. It's not that hard to find campus police officers walking around, no matter when. They have routine check-ups on the street as well as in the dorms. Also, they e-mail students whenever there are some events within or around the campus that may affect the campus security, so you should know better than to walk around without being prepared."

Q "Security is normally good, but there are some bad incidents sometimes. I've never heard of anyone getting killed, but I have heard about **attempted rapes** by strangers, and one actual rape. There is a region by the school that is also not that safe, near the University of Pittsburgh. I think as long as you hang out with a large crowd, you should always be fine."

Q "Security is pretty good at CMU, and **I feel safe walking around campus at any time of the day or night**. I usually hang out with friends till the wee hours of the night and I live on the other side of campus. I don't have any problems walking back alone. There are services like campus police and escorts that will pick you up from wherever you are and take you back to your room. We also have Safe Walk, where two students walk with you to wherever you need to go. I think security and safety is well taken care of on campus. Honestly, there have been a few incidents in the past with attempted assaults, but the University quickly responded by having more campus police around."

Q "Pittsburgh makes security a big issue. The **campus police are fairly active**; I see them walking or driving around just about every day. I would say that the biggest issue here is sexual assault. There have been a few security bulletins— two or three over the course of the year—posted about young females being attacked because they were walking alone late at night."

Q "CMU has an interesting security situation. Basically, the University has its own police force. **Campus police are always around** during the day, and especially at night. I feel very safe when I walk to and from class. I mean, it's not a very large campus, so I don't think you have too much to worry about with that. However, I have noticed that there were a lot of assaults—probably four or five— and one mugging, but the campus police handled it very well. They post you with up-to-date information on where to be careful and places to avoid; I wouldn't sweat it."

Q "Well, **there were a few attempted robberies, but they all failed**. As a result, however, they're trying to add more emergency phones around; there aren't enough right now. There's a group called Safe Walk, and they will send two escorts to walk you at night. Also, there were very few safety breaches within the dorm."

The College Prowler Take On...
Safety & Security

Although there is crime on and around campus, students are in agreement that they feel secure and not too concerned about their safety. Campus initiatives like Safe Walk and the escort van service have really helped students feel safer. Two police cars and one supervisor patrol the campus 24 hours a day. Dorm security, however, is very lax. Quickly flashing your ID at the entrance to any dorm is enough to get you, all your friends, and that garbage bag filled with beer that you're holding into the building. Recent efforts to monitor who comes in and out of the dorms have been largely unsuccessful, due to the fact that the desk attendant position is student-run. Complaints about bikes are well-founded, too. It is very common to see the dismembered handlebars and spokes of bikes that have been destroyed still chained to the rack. Whoever has a passion for destroying these bikes is still pretty much a mystery.

The CMU police should also be commended for maintaining a highly visible presence and giving the campus such a safe feel. Because of the campus' polished, professional atmosphere, it's easy to forget that walking just a few blocks off campus could possibly put you in a much worse area. However, while there aren't many instances of crime by students, it goes without saying that valuables (laptops) left unprotected or unlocked in a campus locker run a high risk of being stolen.

B+

The College Prowler® Grade on
Safety & Security: B+

A high grade in Safety & Security means that students generally feel safe, campus police are visible, blue light phones and escort services are readily available, and safety precautions are not overly necessary.

Computers

The Lowdown On...
Computers

High-Speed Network?
Yes

Wireless Network?
Yes

Number of Labs:
11

Number of Computers:
356

Operating Systems:
PC, Mac, UNIX

Free Software:
Acrobat Reader

CodeWarrior Corporate Time

Ethernet Campus Network

Maple

Mathematica

Matlab

Minitab

Mulberry

NiftyTelnet

Symantec Antivirus

Visual Studio server

Did You Know?

Carnegie Mellon was **ranked the nation's most wired university** in 2000 and 2001 in a Yahoo! Internet Life study.

Students Speak Out On...
Computers

"Having your own computer is a must. CMU has tons of clusters with all different types of computers—Windows, Mac, UNIX, Sun—but having one in your room is really convenient."

Q "The **wireless network at CMU is extensive**. Basically, if you have a laptop, bring it, and you can access the Internet from anywhere on campus."

Q "It's really convenient to bring your own computer. Sadly, **most freshmen network with other freshmen friends via Instant Messenger**. People check their e-mail every five minutes, so if you want to be a true CMU student, you'd need a computer for that. I'd recommend bringing a laptop, because the school has wireless Internet, so you can sit in class, outside, or in the library and be online. You'll be happier with a laptop, and you won't feel like an outsider!"

Q "**If you can afford a computer, bring one**. If you can't or don't want to, you'll still be fine. Occasionally, your life will be a living hell when everyone has a project due and all the campus printers are acting strange, but you can make it just fine without a computer. The clusters (labs) can get crowded, but if you budget your time well—which you most likely won't—you don't need to sink more cash into a computer."

Q "I think **CMU has more computers per square foot than people**. There are a whole lot of public clusters, and your department will have its own private clusters. You can usually find a computer if you want one."

Q "Computer **labs are usually crowded**, but there are a lot of them, so you'll be fine. Every Sunday night, though, the network goes down for about seven hours."

Q "We are supposedly the most wired campus in the country. We have **17 computer clusters** and now even a wireless network—that means you can use the Internet anywhere on campus; all you need is a wireless Ethernet card. This school is one of the best places to study computers, so we have good facilities for both Macs and PCs. You can usually find an open computer; if you can't in one place, a nearby cluster will have an open one. I have even heard rumors that if an enemy country wanted to drop a nuclear bomb on the U.S., CMU is one of the first targets because the CIA has headquarters and top-secret computers located here! I'm not sure if that's true."

Q "I'd say **we're pretty well-connected**. I'm not sure that it's good enough to be number one, but I think they do a good job. Most people get Ethernet connections, which are really fast. The computer clusters usually have quite a few people in them, but you'll almost always find your own computer to use. The computers at the clusters are fast, because Intel is always donating stuff. I would advise you to bring your own computer, but then again, I'm a computer science major. If you're really into computers, you might prefer to bring a desktop. Pretty much all of the school has a wireless connection, which means you can go on the net from anywhere if you have a laptop. If you don't mind walking a little to get to a cluster, then there's no need to bring a computer."

Q "CMU is like **a planet of computers**. There are literally computers everywhere. There are so many computer clusters all over campus—in academic buildings, in dorms—they're everywhere! They're never really crowded, but I would suggest bringing your own computer for convenience. Our school is very computer-oriented. Professors post notes and homework online; quizzes and problem sets are online. It's just good to have, I guess."

Q "This is considered **the most wired campus in the country** because we were the first school to install a wireless network. I think there are actually more computers than students on this campus, so crowded labs are never a problem. It's not necessary to have your own, although it can be convenient."

Q "**Wireless is a godsend**. There are computers everywhere. Clusters are not all that crowded until you get to the end of the semesters. People prefer to have their own computers. I would suggest getting a laptop since the wireless Ethernet on campus is definitely an advantage. We're all really computer-savvy, so resources are normally not hard to come by. You can even rent laptop computers from the business school and the University Center for hours at a time."

The College Prowler Take On...
Computers

Yes, the wireless Ethernet network is great, but it shouldn't overshadow the sheer volume of computers and computer supplies around campus. With so many computers, it's no surprise that students rarely have a problem finding an open computer in the cluster. It's true that many classes utilize the Blackboard Web site to post homework assignments, announcements, and grades. For some courses, students may have to check this site almost every day. The constant need to check your e-mail is another endearingly nerdy characteristic about CMU, and some students will start to get antsy if they can't access their accounts. There's a good reason for this, however, since professors will often e-mail students with news about class.

The campus is so computer-focused that it can be a little overbearing for the mouse-wielding novice. Eventually, though, every student gets up to speed. If you can afford to bring a computer, then make sure you bring one, and make sure it's new. Technology becomes outdated even faster at CMU then it does in the real world. For students excited by the wireless network, a good laptop can be indispensable. When selecting a wireless card, however, make sure to buy the University-recommended card; it'll make getting on the campus network a lot easier for you. Computers are more than just machines at CMU; they're a way of life. You haven't experienced computer culture until you've come here.

The College Prowler® Grade on

Computers: A+

A high grade in Computers designates that computer labs are available, the computer network is easily accessible, and the campus' computing technology is up to date.

Facilities

The Lowdown On...
Facilities

Student Center:
The University Center (The UC)

Libraries:
Engineering and Science Library
Hunt Library
Mellon Institute Library
Posner Center
Software Engineering Institute Library
Universal Digital Library

Athletic Center:
The UC Gym
Skibo Gymnasium

Popular Place to Chill:
Skibo Coffee House
The UC
The Fence

What Is There to Do On Campus?

Between classes you can break a sweat in the gym, cool off in the pool, take in a play, grab a bite to eat, or settle down to a $1 movie without ever leaving campus.

Movie Theater on Campus?

Yes; McConomy Auditorium, the University Center

Bowling on Campus?

No

Bar on Campus?

No, although Panther Hollow Inn (PHI) is right down the street.

Coffeehouse on Campus?

Yes. Skibo Coffeehouse, the University Center

Favorite Things to Do

The school shows a lot of movies, and these are very popular with students looking to relax for a few hours. Plays in the Purnell Center often draw larger crowds than most football games, and there's always someone in the computer clusters—whether they're doing work or playing a game. Skibo Coffeehouse often holds student readings and open mic nights, and Rangos Hall (in the University Center) is host to concerts, guest speakers, dance competitions, and fashion shows.

Students Speak Out On...
Facilities

{ **"There are a couple of gyms that are okay. We have all the fields and facilities you could really want, and they do the job even if they aren't billion-dollar facilities."**

Q "The athletic facilities are mediocre. The track and football field have all-weather turf, which is nice. The **student center is big**, and it has a movie theater, a bookstore, a ton of clubs, a radio station, a pool, a gym, five squash and racquetball courts, an aerobics room, a large stage for events, and many places to eat (but those get old pretty fast)."

Q "CMU has **the cleanest bathrooms** of any school I've ever seen. They're not cushy, but they're nice."

Q "Mostly **everything on campus seems to be newly-remodeled**. Since we have such a big computer department at our school, computer companies fight to give us computers. We have brand-new Macs and IBMs in all the labs. The gym is pretty nice, but if you are a hardcore athlete and you work out a lot, you may have to wait for a machine once in a while."

Q "The computer places are good. I've never used the athletic stuff, although they seem decent for a fairly un-athletic school. Part of CMU's problem is that **it doesn't have one main gathering area for students** to meet and build a student community. Therefore, school unity suffers and the school becomes segregated into cliques which mingle on occasion."

Q "They show **movies in the University Center** on a big screen for $1; that's always nice."

Q "The UC is a place to come hang out, but as of right now, **there's not too much to do** there besides relax and eat."

Q "The athletic facilities are very nice. We have a 25-meter pool, track, football field, and other things. Overall, the campus layout is nice because **everything is very close**, but housing services is very lacking in the speed with which they fix things."

Q "The gym is nice, although it gets pretty crowded during peak hours. **I think CMU should definitely spend more money** on its facilities."

Q "**The weight room is small**, but the University Center offers some exercise classes you can take. I find that it all suits my needs. I just take a few aerobics classes a week. The University Center has a small bookstore and a convenience store, both open fairly late. There's limited stuff, but it's sufficient."

Q "**We have a very nice swimming pool**, indoor racquetball/squash courts, tennis courts, and a football field. We also have a nice student center."

Q "I think the facilities are pretty nice. **There is always construction being done on campus** because they're always trying to improve what we have. The architecture is a little weird, but it's huge, new, and inviting. Computers are always state-of-the-art, and I swear that there are more of them than there are students."

The College Prowler Take On...
Facilities

The University Center is the focal point of campus life at CMU. It contains numerous eateries, a gym, basketball court, and meeting rooms. It's also a great place to just sit and chill between classes. The UC is only a few years old, and the building itself is an impressive piece of architecture. Athletic facilities in the UC include an enormous basketball court/gymnasium, a small but adequate weight room, five racquetball courts, and an aerobics room. Skibo Gym, a larger athletic facility, is also located on campus. Skibo is an old, poorly-maintained gym that attracts dedicated weightlifters.

On the whole, the campus is aesthetically pleasing. Some students have even said that the College of Fine Arts building is the reason that they came to Carnegie Mellon. It is a stunning structure to be enjoyed by all students, but it's casual yet austere air is most compatible with art, design, and architecture majors. There are also some buildings that reflect the campus' industrial bent. The dank and stale Wean Hall is the largest poured concrete building in the country. It's also one of the most repulsive, but you won't see that on any fact sheets. It's recommended to tour the campus before attending CMU. Most prospective students are charmed by its quaint yet busy atmosphere, but some find the buildings to be a bit ugly.

B-

The College Prowler® Grade on

Facilities: B-

A high Facilities grade indicates that the campus is aesthetically pleasing and well maintained, facilities are state-of-the-art, and libraries are exceptional. Other determining factors include the quality of both athletic and student centers and an abundance of things to do on campus.

Campus Dining

The Lowdown On...
Campus Dining

Freshman Meal Plan Requirement?
Yes

Meal Plan Average Cost:
$3,650

Places to Grab a Bite with Your Meal Plan:

Andy's
Location: UC
Food: wraps, smoothies
Favorite Dish: the Beeler turkey wrap
Hours: Monday–Friday 8 a.m.–8 p.m.

→

Asiana

Location: Newell-Simon

Food: Chinese

Favorite Dish: BarbeGrill Chicken

Hours: Monday–Friday 11 a.m.-7 p.m.

Barista Café

Location: UC

Food: Coffee/bakery

Favorite Dish: Bagel with flavored cream cheese

Hours: Monday–Friday 8 a.m.–10:30 a.m.

Bento Bowl

Location: UC

Food: Asian

Favorite Dish: Shrimp lo mein

Hours: Monday–Thursday 11 a.m.–4 p.m., Friday 11 a.m.–7 p.m.

CK's Pretzels

Location: UC

Food: Pretzels, cookies, and shakes

Favorite Dish: Pepperoni and provalone pretzel sandwich

Hours: Monday–Friday 10 a.m.–7 p.m., Saturday 11 a.m.–5 p.m.

East Street Deli

Location: UC

Food: Sandwiches/breakfast

Favorite Dish: Smoked turkey sandwich

Hours: Monday–Friday 10:30 a.m.–4 p.m.

Ginger's Coffeehouse

Location: Baker Hall and Purnell Center

Food: Coffee, sandwiches

Favorite Dish: Cappuccino

Hours: Monday–Friday 8 a.m.–4 p.m. (Purnell closes at 3 p.m. on Fridays)

Ginger's Deli

Location: Posner Hall

Food: Sandwiches/soups

Favorite Dish: Hot soup

Hours: Monday–Thursday 8 a.m.–7 p.m., Friday 8 a.m.–3 p.m., Saturday 9 a.m.–2 p.m.

Grab n' Go

Location: UC

Food: Drinks, fruit, chips

Favorite Dish: Iced tea and an apple

Hours: Monday–Friday 11 a.m.–8 p.m., Saturday–Sunday 2 p.m.–8 p.m.

Highlander Café

Location: Resnick House

Food: All-you-can-eat, home-cooked foods, salad station, pizza station, deli

Favorite Dish: Chicken ceasar salad

Hours: Monday–Friday 7:30 a.m.–10 a.m., 11 a.m.–2:30 p.m., 4 p.m.–7 p.m., Saturday–Sunday 11 a.m.–2:30 p.m., 4 p.m.–7 p.m.

Kosher Korner

Location: UC

Food: Kosher meals

Favorite Dish: Kosher salad

Hours: Monday–Friday 11 a.m.–8 p.m., Saturday–Sunday 2 p.m.–8 p.m.

La Prima

Location: Wean Hall

Food: Drinks, sandwiches, cookies, muffins

Favorite Dish: Focaccia pizza bread

Hours: Monday–Friday 8 a.m.–4 p.m.

Main Street Market

Location: Newell-Simon

Food: Salads, sandwiches, pizza, soup

Favorite Dish: Cheese tortellini

Hours: Monday–Friday 8 a.m.–3 p.m.

The Original Hot Dog Shop

Location: UC

Food: Fries, subs, hot dogs

Favorite Dish: Cheese dog with fries

Hours: Daily 11 a.m.–2 a.m.

Pennes International Marketplace

Location: UC

Food: Home-cooked meals

Favorite Dish: Chicken cacciatore

Hours: Monday–Friday 11 a.m.–2 p.m.

Pepperazi

Location: UC

Food: Italian

Favorite Dish: Baked pasta with cheese

Hours: Monday–Friday 11 a.m.–4 p.m.

Schatz All-You-Care-to-Eat

Location: UC

Food: chicken, Stir-fry

Favorite Dish: Hamburger

Hours: Monday–Thursday 7:30 a.m.–10:30 a.m., 5 p.m.–8 p.m., Friday 7:30 a.m.–10:30 a.m., Saturday–Sunday 10:30 a.m.–2 p.m.

Schatz Dining Hall

Location: UC

Food: Buffet-style

Favorite Dish: Grilled cheese

Hours: Monday–Friday
11 a.m.–2 p.m.

Showcase Salads

Location: UC

Food: Made-to-go salads

Favorite Dish: Thai
noodle salad

Hours: Monday–Friday
11 a.m.–8 p.m., Saturday–
Sunday 2 p.m.–8 p.m.

Si Señor

Location: UC

Food: Southwest/Mexican

Favorite Dish: Chicken
cilantro quesadilla

Hours: Daily 11 a.m.–10 p.m.

Skibo Coffeehouse

Location: UC

Food: Coffee, pastries

Favorite Dish: Mocha, cookie

Hours: Monday–Friday
9 a.m.–11 p.m., Saturday–
Sunday 8 a.m.–11 p.m.

Taste of India

Location: 4902 Forbes
Abenue and Resnik House

Food: Indian

Favorite Dish: Chicken curry

Hours: Forbes, Monday–
Friday 11 a.m.–2 p.m.;
Resnick, Daily 5 p.m.–9 p.m.

The Underground

Location: Morewood E-Tower

Food: Sandwiches, soups

Favorite Dish: Cheeseburger

Hours: Monday–Friday
8:30 a.m.–11 p.m., Saturday–
Sunday 9 a.m.–11 p.m.

The Zebra Lounge

Location: College of Fine Arts

Food: Coffee, cookies

Favorite Dish: Hot chocolate,
and scones

Hours: Monday–Friday
8 a.m.–5 p.m.

Student Favorites:

The Original Hot Dog Shop

Si Señor

Taste of India

Off-Campus Places to Use DineXtra:

Eat'n Park
1816 Murray Ave.,
Squirrel Hill
(412) 422-7203

The Original Hot Dog Shop
3901 Forbes Ave.,
Oakland
(412) 621-7388

Vocelli Pizza
3608 Fifth Ave.,
Oakland
(412) 687-4666

Subway
415 S. Craig St.,
Oakland
(412) 687-6728

24-Hour On-Campus Eating?
No

Other Options

Many students choose to eat at privately-owned trucks parked outside of Posner Hall. These trucks offer Chinese, Thai, Mediterranean, Mexican, and Indian food at a low price and remain to be one of the most popular options around campus.

Did You Know?

Ever go traying? When it snows, **CMU kids will steal the cafeteria trays and use them to go sled riding** on the hills behind Donner Hall and in Schenley Park.

Students Speak Out On...
Campus Dining

"The thing I dislike the most about CMU is that there is no central dining hall. As a freshman, I thought the food was okay. As a sophomore, I got sick of it pretty quickly and started eating off campus a lot."

Q "The food is **overpriced and causes malnutrition**. It's impossible to eat enough on campus if you're vegetarian or keeping kosher."

Q "Food is okay. **If you are a vegetarian, you may have some qualms**, but check out Si Señor. I ate there every night my freshman year. Skibo has a lot of healthy food and veggie food; it also plays music and achieves a college coffeehouse atmosphere. I recommend checking it out. Usually, people decide to come to CMU just because of Skibo. It's those same students who end up working there and creating their own smoothies. There's also an all-you-can-eat buffet some nights each week, if you want to gorge. The Underground is only an okay place to eat, but it's a very cool place to hang out. It's under Morewood—a freshman dorm—so that's a convenient place."

Q "Since I'm in my fifth year, I don't know how the food is anymore, but I hear **it has gotten a lot better**. Posner Hall has a place to eat which is good; it has sandwiches and soups and two different hot meals each day. The University Center food is all right; it really depends on what you like. There is a large variety: Mexican, American, Middle Eastern, Italian, chicken, and bagels."

Q "**The food sucks**. The school has made a huge effort to diversify the selection of food, and in the process has made it so confusing and crappy that being on the meal plan is a hassle. You look forward to the times of day when you don't have to eat at the irritating establishments around campus. The meal plan is of poor value, overly complicated, and worst of all, it's very unsatisfying because the food is always too greasy, too bland, too overcooked, or too weird. The Chinese restaurant in Newell-Simon is one of the better spots, and sometimes the pizza in the University Center is good. The best dining on campus is the selection of vans parked next to Posner Hall—there's Chinese, Thai, Greek, and Indian. It's all fresh and fairly tasty and at a very good value."

Q "The food is okay on campus, although **it's a little expensive** through the required first-year meal plan. It is varied. We have Indian, Chinese, Italian, and Mexican, as well as sandwiches, pizza, and normal American food. I'm happy with the meal situation here, although I'm not very picky."

Q "The food on campus sucks, for the most part. **I eat mostly off campus, or food I cook myself**. There is stuff in the University Center that is good for snacking and some are at reasonable prices, but a lot of it is overpriced. Personally, if I have to eat on campus, I will eat at one of two places. This guy named Sree sells Indian food out of a van over by Posner Hall; I know that sounds bad, but a lot of people do it. It's good food, you get a lot of it, and it's cheap—four bucks gets you a fairly large meal and a drink. You can't beat that!"

Q "**The food on campus really sucks**, and I'm sure most people will tell you that. If you come, get as few meal plans as possible with money to spend wherever. Anyways, most people skip some meals and have a lot of their weekly plan leftover by Sunday. It doesn't carry over, so I bought a giant pack of orange juice the last day because I had so much left over that I needed to spend it."

Q "**I don't know anyone who likes the food on campus**, and they make you eat on campus for the first year. This can be either bad or good. It's bad because you're forced to pay high prices and eat their food. It's good because you won't be starved and there's a very good chance that you'll eat more than you would otherwise. Regardless, after the first year, you can get off the school plan (which is what everyone does) and then use your money however you want. It's always nice to go to someplace close to school where you can eat well."

Q "Food is surprisingly really good at CMU. I've visited a lot of my friends at other colleges and their food just sucks. **We have a wide variety**, ranging from Mexican food, to a deli, to fried food, and also Indian and Chinese food. We pretty much have everything, and it's not bad at all."

Q "I think every school has its ups and downs with food. **The food at CMU is relatively good**. It all tastes good. I'm not sure how healthy some of the food is, but I think everyone finds something decent. After a while, I found that I get really tired of having the same food over and over. Usually, students end their meal plan after the first year; I'm staying on it. The meal plan goes like this: you have a certain number of blocks, and then you have a certain amount of DineXtra (basically, it's money you can use at anytime on campus until you run out)."

Q "There are little trucks that sit in the street on campus, and those are the places to hit up for lunch—it's mostly Chinese, Thai, etc. It's pretty good food! Other than that, there are places to eat on campus, but there are so many places to walk to, **I'd rather go off campus**."

Q "The campus dining experience **leaves a lot to be desired**. Food plans have changed a lot since I've been there, but you need to go for the plan that gives you the most flexibility—DineXtra is much better than meal blocks. The many food carts around the streets are very popular. Sree's Indian food is probably the best of these."

The College Prowler Take On...
Campus Dining

All but the most optimistic students have problems with campus dining. Fixing the dining situation is a big problem for the University, and an even bigger hassle for the students; campus dining consists of individual campus-run restaurants rather than large, central dining halls. The meal plan provides you with two ways to pay. A "block" is a unit of credit that's good for one whole meal. The other way to pay, DineXtra, works like cash; it can be used at all Dining Services locations, as well as four off-campus restaurants. The average meal will cost you about $7. Freshmen are required to be on the meal plan, and most are unhappy with it. Fortunately, students can structure their meal plan to provide themselves with the most flexibility by choosing how much money to allot to block units and how much money to allot to DineXtra.

The most disappointing thing about eating on campus is the small amount of food you receive for the high price you pay. The food isn't all bad. A dining hall would be nice, but the lack of one means that CMU students don't have to suffer through cafeteria-style food. Asiana and Si Señor offer some delicious dishes, and the Original Hot Dog Shop offers some of the tastiest artery-clogging food in town. For freshman year, the meal plan is bearable, but after that, most students stay off campus when grabbing a bite to eat.

The College Prowler® Grade on

Campus Dining: C-

Our grade on Campus Dining addresses the quality of both school-owned dining halls and independent on campus restaurants as well as the price, availability, and variety of food available.

Off-Campus Dining

The Lowdown On...
Off-Campus Dining

Restaurant Prowler:
Popular Places to Eat!

Buffalo Blues
216 S. Highland Ave., Shadyside
(412) 362-5837
Food: American/BBQ
Cool Features: Two floors/ sports bar
Price: $10 and under per person
Monday–Saturday 11 a.m.– 2 a.m., Sunday 12 p.m.–2 a.m

Casbah
229 S. Highland Ave., Shadyside
(412) 661-5656
Food: Italian/Mediterranean
Cool Features: Extensive wine list
Price: $25 and under per person
Monday–Thursday 11:30 a.m.–2:30 p.m., 5 p.m.–10 p.m., Friday 11:30 a.m.–2:30 p.m., 5 p.m.–11 p.m., Saturday 5 p.m.–11 p.m., Sunday 11 a.m.–2 p.m., 5 p.m.–9 p.m.

➜

China Palace

5440 Walnut St.,
Shadyside

(412) 687-RICE

*http://chinapalacepittsburgh
.com*

Cool Features: Bar

Food: Chinese

Price: $15 and under
per person

Hours: Monday–Thursday
11:30 a.m.–10 p.m., Friday–
Saturday 11:30 a.m.–11 p.m.,
Sunday 2 p.m.–9 p.m.

Cozumel

5505 Walnut St.,
Shadyside

(412) 621-5100

Food: Mexican

Cool Features: Dancing

Price: $15 and under
per person

Hours: Monday–Friday
11 a.m.–2:30 p.m., 5 p.m.–
10 p.m., Saturday 12 p.m.–
10 p.m., Sunday 12 p.m.–
9 p.m.

Eat'n Park

1816 Murray Ave.,
Squirrel Hill

(412) 422-7203

www.eatnpark.com

Food: American

Cool Features: Smiley
face cookies, open 24 hours

Price: $15 and under
per person

Hours: Daily 24 hours

Fuel & Fuddle

212 Oakland Ave.,
Oakland

(412) 682-3473

www.fuelandfuddle.com

Food: American

Cool Features: Live music,
poetry readings, extensive
beer selection

Price: $15 and under
per person

Hours: Daily 11 a.m.–2 a.m.

India Garden

328 Atwood St.,
Oakland

(412) 682-3000

www.indiagarden.net

Food: Indian

Price: $15 and under
per person

Hours: Daily 11 a.m.–1 a.m.

Joe Mama's

3716 Forbes Ave.,
Oakland

(412) 621-7282

Food: Italian

Price: $15 and under
per person

Hours: Monday–Saturday
11 a.m.–11 p.m., Sunday
4 a.m.–11 p.m.

Bar: Daily until 2 a.m.

Lucca

317 S. Craig St.,
Oakland

(412) 682-3310

(Lucca, continued)

Food: Italian

Cool Features: Candle-lit patio dining

Price: $35 and under per person

Hours: Daily 11 a.m.– 9:30 p.m.

LuLu's Noodle Shop

400 S. Craig St., Oakland

(412) 681-3333

Food: Asian

Price: $15 and under per person

Hours: Daily 11 a.m.– 9:30 p.m.

Mad Mex

370 Atwood St., Oakland

(412) 681-5656

www.madmex.com

Food: Mexican

Cool Features: Huge margaritas

Price: $10 and under per person

Hours: Daily 11 a.m.–1 a.m.

Max and Erma's

5533 Walnut St., Shadyside

(412) 681-5775

www.maxandermas.com

Food: American

Price: $15 and under per person

(Max and Erma's, continued)

Hours: Sunday–Thursday 11:30 a.m.–10 p.m., Friday– Saturday 11:30 a.m.–11 p.m.

Monterey Bay Fish Grotto

1411 Grandview Ave., Mount Washington

(412) 481-4414

http://montereybayfish grotto.com

Food: Seafood

Cool Features: Great city view

Price: $35 and under per person

Hours: Monday–Thursday 11 a.m.–10 p.m., Friday 11 a.m.–12 a.m., Saturday 4 p.m.–10 p.m.

New Dumpling House

2138 Murray Ave., Squirrel Hill

(412) 422-4178

Food: Chinese/Japanese

Price: $15 and under per person

Hours: Monday–Thursday 11 a.m.–10 p.m., Friday– Saturday 11 a.m.–10 p.m., Sunday 11 a.m.–10 p.m.

Orient Kitchen

4808 Baum Blvd., Shadyside

(412) 682-3311

Food: Asian

Price: $15 and under per person

(Orient Kitchen, continued)
Hours: Sunday–Thursday
11 a.m.–1 a.m., Friday–
Saturday 11 a.m.–2 a.m

Pamela's
3703 Forbes Ave,
Oakland
(412) 683-4066
Food: Breakfast
Price: $10 and under
per person
Hours: Daily 7:30 a.m.–5 p.m.

Pino's Mercato
6738 Reynolds St.,
Point Breeze
(412) 661-3651
Food: Italian
Price: $15 and under
per person
Hours: Monday 11 a.m.–
9 p.m., Tuesday–Friday
11 a.m.–10 p.m.,
Saturday 12 p.m.–10 p.m.,
Sunday 4 p.m.–9 p.m.

Pittsburgh Deli Company
728 Copeland St.,
Shadyside
(412) 682-3354
Food: Sandwiches
Cool Features: Half-off menu
Sunday–Thursday 10 p.m.–
12 a.m.
Price: $10 and under
per person
Hours: Daily 11 a.m.–2 a.m.

Primanti Brothers
3803 Forbes Ave.,
Oakland
(412) 621-4444
www.primantibros.com
Food: American/fast food
Price: $10 and under
per person
Hours: Monday–Saturday
10 a.m.–2 a.m.,
Sunday 11 a.m.–12 a.m.

Ritters
5221 Baum Blvd.,
North Oakland
(412) 682-4852
Food: Diner
Price: $12 and under
per person
Hours: Daily 24 hours

Sushi Too
5432 Walnut St.,
Shadyside
(412) 687-8744
www.sushi2-too.com
Food: Japanese
Cool Features: Traditional
Japenese atmosphere
Price: $15 and under
per person
Hours: Monday–Thursday
11:30 a.m.–3 p.m.,
5 p.m.–10 p.m., Friday 11:30
a.m.–3 p.m., 5 p.m.–11 p.m.,
Saturday 11:30 a.m.–11 p.m.,
Sunday 1 p.m.–9 p.m.

Thai Place Café
301 S. Craig St.,
Oakland
(412) 622-0133
www.thaiplacepgh.com
Food: Thai
Price: $15 and under
per person
Hours: Monday–Saturday
10:30 a.m.–9:30 p.m.

Tom's Diner
1715 E Carson St,
South Side
(412) 488-0900
Food: American
Cool Features: '50s retro
atmosphere
Price: $10 and under
per person
Hours: Daily 24 hours

Union Grill
413 S. Craig St., Oakland
(412) 681-8620
Food: American
Cool Features: outdoor
dining, good happy
hour specials
Price: $15 and under
per person
Hours: Monday–Thursday
11:30 a.m.–10 p.m., Friday–
Saturday 11:30 a.m.–10 p.m.,
Sunday 11:30 a.m.–9 p.m.

Village Pizza
810 Ivy St., Shadyside
(412) 682-6878
Food: American/Italian
Price: $10 and under per
person
Hours: Monday–Tuesday
11 a.m.–2 a.m., Wednesday–
Saturday 11 a.m.–2 a.m.,
Sunday 12 p.m.–2 a.m.

Late-Night, Half-Price Food Specials:
Fuel & Fuddle

India Garden

Joe Mama's

Mad Mex

Pittsburgh Deli Company

24-Hour Eating?
Eat'n Park

Ritter's Diner

Tom's Diner

Other Places to Check Out:
Aladdin's

Craig Street Coffee

Gullifty's

Hemingway's

Pi

Qdoba

Subway

Did You Know?

Big Macs, **Heinz Ketchup**, and Klondike Bars were all invented in Pittsburgh.

Ever have a pierogie? Usually stuffed with potatoes, cheese, or sauerkraut, these dumplings are a Pittsburgh staple thanks to the **city's Polish heritage**.

Want a **Pittsburgh-style salad**? Just add fries.

Closest Grocery Stores:

Giant Eagle
4612 Centre Ave.,
North Oakland
(412) 681-1500

Giant Eagle
4250 Murray Ave.,
Squirrel Hill
(412) 421-8161

Whole Foods
5880 Centre Ave.,
Shadyside
(412) 441-7960

Best Pizza:
Village Pizza

Best Chinese:
LuLu's Noodles

Best Breakfast:
Pamela's

Best Wings:
Buffalo Blues

Best Healthy:
Whole Foods

Best Place to Take Your Parents:
Casbah
Monterey Bay Fish Grotto

Students Speak Out On...
Off-Campus Dining

> "There are a lot of restaurants within close proximity of campus, and there are even more if you are willing to take the bus, which is free for CMU students."

Q "My **favorite place to eat is at the Waterfront**. It's about ten minutes away by bus and has lots of restaurants. Subway, my personal favorite for a quick meal, is very close to campus as well."

Q "**There are a bunch of good eats**. In Oakland, check out Fuel & Fuddle at night; it's half-price after 11 p.m., and it's a real college place. In Squirrel Hill, go to Aladdin's—it has all kinds of Middle Eastern food, and everything on the menu is super tasty. LuLu's is my friend's favorite place; sometimes he eats there several times a day. It's pretty close to campus and has Pan-Asian food, whatever that means. Craig Street Coffee is pretty good, too!"

Q "Restaurants off campus are decent. Sometimes **it can be frustrating to eat pizza and subs all the time**, but truthfully, the CMU area of Pittsburgh has some pretty affordable places to eat where things don't taste too bad."

Q "**Restaurants with waiters and waitresses don't exist on campus**, but off-campus, at the University of Pittsburgh in Oakland (a ten-minute walk from CMU), there are a bunch of good restaurants. Fuel & Fuddle and Mad Mex are half-price after 11 p.m., which is a big thing for students."

Q "We're right in a city, so **eating off campus is great**. There are three neighborhoods around us with great places: Oakland, Squirrel Hill, and Shadyside. Craig Street is right by campus and has lots of great places. I don't like to recommend one restaurant because I'm all about experimenting."

Q "I found that a lot of the restaurants off campus are really good; **they have a lot of Indian and Chinese**. The pizza is awful! I guess I'm just spoiled, coming from New York and all. Oh my God, go to LuLu's! It's the best Chinese food I have ever had! Pino's and Gullifty's are really good places. Joe Mama's and Fuel & Fuddle have half-off food nights, as well."

Q "There are lots of great places in Pittsburgh; the city is as diverse as the school. In fact, I go to new places all the time. **Pittsburgh really has everything**. You can even get Kosher Chinese food."

Q "The restaurants aren't bad. There's fast food all over the place. In addition, there are Italian places called Pi and Pino's in Squirrel Hill, an American place in Shadyside called Max and Erma's, **some fun places in Oakland where you can get half-priced food**, and lots of yummy places downtown. There is really a wide spectrum of stuff."

Q "**Hemingway's has half-price food** between 9 p.m. and 12 a.m., and LuLu's is not that expensive. You can eat the old fast food stuff, but I guess there's nothing new about that."

The College Prowler Take On...
Off-Campus Dining

Off-campus dining provides students with a diverse array of foods to choose from. Just about every student has his own favorite restaurant. It's hard for students to decide exactly where to eat, with so many delectable dining options available. Students love places that offer half-price dining (Fuel & Fuddle, Joe Mama's, India Garden, Pittsburgh Deli Company, Hemingway's, and Mad Mex). Not only do these establishments offer students great prices, but their culinary creations are plentiful and delicious. Most students agree that LuLu's is the best Chinese food in the area. The amount of food you get for the price you pay is very generous. Sushi Too in Shadyside is a great place for all kinds of Japanese food, not just sushi, and right down the street at Cozumel you can find a lively environment and some spicy Mexican cuisine. Leaving the campus to dine out is a joy for most students!

Compared with the extremely poor condition of on-campus dining, eating off-campus becomes even more appealing. If there's one downside, it's that students are usually too busy to leave campus for an enjoyable sit-down meal. As a student, you may find yourself eating at one place over and over again simply because it's convenient; make an attempt to explore the local dining scene, as it can yield some sumptuous results.

A-

The College Prowler® Grade on
Off-Campus
Dining: A-

A high Off Campus Dining grade implies that off campus restaurants are affordable, accessible, and worth visiting. Other factors include the variety of cuisine and the availability of alternative options (vegetarian, vegan, kosher, etc.).

Campus Housing

The Lowdown On...
Campus Housing

Room Types:

Residence rooms include standard, prime, suite-style units, apartment-style units

Best Dorms:

Morewood Gardens

Mudge House

New House

Resnik

West Wing

Worst Dorms:

Scobell

Boss

Donner

Hamerschlag

Undergrads on Campus:

72%

→

Dormitories:

Boss House

Floors: 3 + basement
Total Occupancy: 72
Bathrooms: In-room
Coed: No
% of Men/Women: 100/0
% of First-Year Students: 48
Room Types: Prime single, prime double
Special Features: Recreation area, television room, study lounge, laundry

Cathedral Mansions

Floors: 9
Total Occupancy: 165
Bathrooms: In-room
Coed: Yes
% of Men/Women: 56/44
% of First-Year Students: 24
Room Types: Efficiency, 1-bedroom, 2-bedroom
Features: Kitchen, laundry

Doherty Apartments

Floors: 3 + basement
Total Occupancy: 53
Bathrooms: In-room
Coed: Yes
% of Men/Women: 44/56
% of First-Year Students: 8
Room Types: Efficiency, 1 Bedroom, 2 Bedroom
Special Features: Recreation area, Ttelevision room, laundry, fitness room

Donner House

Floors: 3 + A level
Total Occupancy: 249
Bathrooms: Shared by floor
Coed: Yes
% of Men/Women: 63/37
% of First-Year Students: 78
Room Types: Standard single, standard double, standard triple
Special Features: Recreation area, television room, study lounge, laundry, kitchen

Fairfax Apartments

Floors: 9
Total Occupancy: 151
Bathrooms: In-room
Coed: Yes
% of Men/Women: 48/52
% of First-Year Students: 7
Room Types: Efficiency, 1-bedroom, 2-bedroom
Features: Kitchen, laundry, workout room

Hamerschlag House

Floors: 3
Total Occupancy: 168
Bathrooms: Shared by Floor
Coed: No
% of Men/Women: 100/0
% of First-Year Students: 96
Room Types: Standard single, prime single, standard double
Special Features: Television/recreation area, common kitchen, laundry, pool table

Henderson House

Floors: 3 + ground level

Total Occupancy: 60

Bathrooms: In-room

Coed: Yes

% of Men/Women: 62/38

% of First-Year Students: 30

Room Types: Prime single, prime double

Special Features: Recreation area, television room, study lounge, laundry, wellness housing

James Manor

Floors: 2

Total Occupancy: 24

Bathrooms: In-room

Coed: Yes

Room Types: 2-bedroom

Features: Kitchen, laundry, 1 parking spot per apartment, fitneess room, social room

London Terrace Apartments

Floors: 3

Total Occupancy: 55

Bathrooms: In-room

Coed: Yes

% of Men/Women: 56/44

% of First-Year Students: 20

Room Types: Efficiency, 1-bedroom

Features: Kitchen, laundry

Margaret Morrison Apartments

Floors: 3

Total Occupancy: 30

Bathroom: Shared by apartment house

Coed: Yes

Room Types: Prime double

Special Features: Only available to students receiving special interest housing, access to computer cluster, laundry, women's center, recreation area

Marybelle Apartments

Floors: 3

Total Occupancy: 34

Bathrooms: In-room

Coed: Yes

% of Men/Women: 68/32

% of First-Year Students: 3

Room Types: Efficiency

Features: Kitchen, laundry

McGill House

Floors: 3 + basement

Total Occupancy: 72

Bathroom: In-room

Coed: No

% of Men/Women: 0/100

% of First-Year Students: 39

Room Types: Prime single, prime double

Special Features: Recreation area, television room, study lounge, laundry

Morewood Gardens A-D Tower

Floors: 7

Total Occupancy: 656

Bathrooms: In-room

Coed: Yes

% of Men/Women: 48/52

% of First-Year Students: 47

Room Types: Efficiency, prime single, prime double, prime triple, prime quad, standard single, standard double

Special Features: Recreation room, television room, study lounge, laundry, computer cluster, mail room, common kitchen

Morewood Gardens E-Tower

Floors: 4

Total Occupancy: 210

Bathrooms: Shared by Floor

Coed: Yes

% of Men/Women: 50/50

% of First-Year Students: 100

Room Types: Standard single, standard double

Special Features: Study lounge, laundry

Mudge House

Floors: 3 + basement

Total Occupancy: 309

Bathrooms: In-room

Coed: Yes

% of Men/Women: 60/40

% of First-Year Students: 42

(Mudge House, continued)

Room Types: House, efficiency, prime single, prime double, prime triple, prime quad, standard single, standard double, standard triple

Features: Living room, dining room, parlor room, study lounge, television room, garden courtyard, laundry, mailroom, common kitchen

New House

Floors: 5

Total Occupancy: 255

Bathrooms: Shared by floor

Coed: Yes

% of Men/Women: 55/45

% of First-Year Students: 96

Room Types: Standard single, standard double

Features: Conference room, laundry, fitness room, study room, recreation area, kitchen, private dining, environmentally-friendly design

Neville Apartments

Floors: 2

Total Occupancy: 22

Bathrooms: In-room

Coed: Yes

Room Types: 1-bedroom, 2-bedroom

Features: Home of the Co-op, an environentally-friendly group

Resnik House

Floors: 5

Total Occupancy: 150

Bathrooms: In-room

Coed: Yes

% of Men/Women: 71/29

% of First-Year Students: 5

Room Types: Prime single, prime double, suites

Features: Air-conditioned, TV room, computer cluster

Roselawn Terrace Houses

Floors: 2 Floors + basement per house

Total Occupancy: 60

Bathrooms: In-house

Coed: Yes

% of Men/Women: 58/42

% of First-Year Students: 7

Room Types: 5-person houses

Features: 3 bedrooms, kitchen, living room, dining room, laundry

Saxony Apartments

Floors: 5

Total Occupancy: 44

Bathrooms: In-room

Coed: Yes

Room Types: Efficiency, 1-bedroom, 2-bedroom

Features: Kitchen, laundry, garage parking (additional charge), some balconies

Scobell House

Floors: 3 + A-level

Total Occupancy: 82

Bathrooms: Shared by floor

Coed: No

% of Men/Women: 100/0

% of First-Year Students: 63

Room Types: Standard single, standard double, prime single

Features: Lounge, laundry

Shady Oak Apartments

Floors: 4

Total Occupancy: 71

Bathrooms: In-room

Coed: Yes

% of Men/Women: 57/43

% of First-Year Students: 1

Room Types: Efficiency, 1-bedroom, 2-bedroom

Features: Kitchen, laundry

Shirley Apartments

Total Occupancy: 41

Bathrooms: In-room

Coed: Yes

% of Men/Women: 34/66

% of First-Year Students: 32

Room Types: Efficiency, 1-bedroom, prime single

Features: Kitchen, laundry

Webster Apartments

Floors: 12

Total Occupancy: 118

Bathrooms: In-room

Coed: Yes

% of Men/Women: 61/39

% of First-Year Students: 17

Room Types: 1-bedroom, 2-bedroom

Features: Kitchen, laundry

Welch House

Floors: 3

Total Occupancy: 56

Bathrooms: In-room

Coed: Yes

% of Men/Women: 52/48

% of First-Year Students: 34

Room Types: Prime single, prime double

Features: Television and study lounge, parlor room, laundry, quiet living area

West Wing

Floors: 5

Total Occupancy: 144

Bathrooms: In-room

Coed: Yes

% of Men/Women: 58/42

% of First-Year Students: 6

Room Types: Prime single, prime double, suite single, suite double

Features: Air-conditioned, television room, computer cluster, mail room

Woodlawn Apartments

Floors: 3 Floors + basement

Total Occupancy: 36

Bathrooms: In-room

Coed: Yes

% of Men/Women: 56/44

% of First-Year Students: 11

Room Types: 1-bedroom, 2-bedroom, 4-bedroom

Features: laundry, art gallery

Did You Know?

All campus residents get **free cable and access to CMU's movie channel**.

CMU has **campus residences for Greek organizations**: Fraternity Quadrangle and the Margaret Morrison Sorority House.

Room Types

Standard – students share a large central bathroom facility (most first-year students are assigned to these rooms).

Prime – students share a private or semi-private bathroom with no more than five students.

Suite-style – students share a semi-private bathroom and a common living area.

Apartments – located both on and off campus. These units can be efficiencies, one-bedrooms or two-bedroom apartments and have in-room kitchens.

Houses – mostly on campus and include bedrooms, a kitchen, dining rooms, living rooms, private bathrooms, and laundry facilities. Many are reserved for special interests or associations.

Bed Type

Twin extra-long (39"x80"); some lofts, some bunk-beds

Available for Rent

Mini fridge with microwave

Cleaning Service?

Yes, in public areas. Community and semi-private bathrooms are cleaned by staff approximately once a week. Community apartment bathrooms are not cleaned.

You Get

Bed, desk and chair, bookshelf, dresser, closet or wardrobe, window coverings, cable TV jack, Ethernet or broadband Internet connections, free campus and local phone calls.

Also Available

Smoke-free living option, special-interest housing

Students Speak Out On...
Campus Housing

{

"The dorms are okay, but most are too small. It's hard to get your own single with your own kitchen and bathroom."

Q "The dorms are pretty nice here. For freshmen, Morewood E-Tower and New House are really nice, but they have communal bathrooms. Mudge is great because it's mostly first-years and you share a bathroom with one other person. **Donner is . . . ugly**."

Q "The dorms are really nice. There is a new dorm (New House) that is LEED certified—that is a rating system for environmental or green buildings. Morewood E-Tower is all freshmen. There are food and mail rooms in that dorm. Mudge is nice, and it's only a bit further away from campus than Morewood. Donner is all freshmen, too, but **stay away from the basement; they call it the Dungeon**."

Q "The dorms are just okay. Supposedly they're much larger than other school's dorms. They're still real crusty though. Do not live in Donner! It is a **stinking cesspool**. Morewood is decent, along with Mudge and Doherty apartments. Get off campus and into local apartments or houses as soon as possible."

Q "Donner is a great dorm for first-years to meet people and be social, but there are community showers and whatnot. Some don't like that, and the fact that the building is green. **Morewood is cool, because a lot of people live there**. E-Tower is for freshmen. Resnik is awful for freshmen."

Q "Morewood and Mudge are nice because they are coed and near the fraternity quad. Donner looks good on the inside, but it's pretty ugly on the outside; it's coed as well. **Stay away from the Hill dorms**: Boss, McGill, Hamerschlag, and Scobell."

Q "The dorms are fine. I lived in Donner Hall my freshman year and had an on-campus apartment sophomore year. **I loved living in Donner**. At first, I was wary of community bathrooms, but it was actually pretty cool, because Donner's where I met my best friends. Sometimes the different majors can be isolated, especially in the College of Fine Arts, so it was great to get to know students from all departments. In fact, my current roommate is a lovely civil engineering major, someone I would never have met if I didn't live in a standard double my first year. That's what I recommend as a first-year student. Living in prime housing (where you share a bathroom with two or three other people) doesn't help you meet other kids. Once you know people, you can move into an apartment of prime rooms. I recommend Donner Hall; it has the biggest rooms and the best sense of community of any of the dorms."

Q "I was in an off-campus apartment called Shirley for the first two weeks. **It was rough**, because of the distance and being in an environment with, like, 38 out of 41 people who were upperclassmen. Now I'm in Morewood, and it's great. Anything on campus is good. Don't request Donner; that's a crappy dorm."

Q "In general, **the dorms are decent**. There aren't many singles, so get used to the idea that you're going to have a roommate. The only freshman dorm that I'd stay away from is Donner because they have a public potty and it looks like a gym on the inside."

Q "**Resnik and West Wing are the best dorms**, I think. But they're usually taken over by juniors and seniors, so it's almost impossible to get in there, especially if you're a freshman. I think Mudge House is pretty neat, but it's, like, ten minutes across the street from the center of the campus, so it's a little farther than I'd like. It looks nice. I suggest you avoid Donner Hall and Hamerschlag House. Hamerschlag is all-male. Although I would hate to live in Donner, I think people learn to live with it in time."

Q "Stay away from Donner. **Morewood sucks, too**, but that's the best chance you have of getting laid at 3 a.m. when you're walking back home drunk from a party. Most freshmen live in Morewood because of that."

The College Prowler Take On...
Campus Housing

All freshmen are required to live on campus. Most students are thankful for their experience in the dorms and feel that they wouldn't have adjusted well to life at CMU without it. It's hard to find a freshman that lived in Morewood E-Tower (a first-year dorm) and didn't have a great time. E-Tower can sometimes seem like the social nexus of the freshman universe. Students from other dorms will even come over just to hang out. Reactions to another freshman-filled dorm, Donner, are mixed. Residents of Donner often build an unflinching solidarity and love for "Big Blue." Students who've stayed elsewhere, however, just find the dormitory to be an eyesore. Community apartment housing is fully-furnished, equipped with a kitchen, and close to campus, but freshmen who've been placed there often express feelings of being out of the social loop.

The dorms are inviting and well-furnished, especially compared to most other colleges and universities. The bathrooms are sufficient, and the showers are spacious. The beds aren't uncomfortable either, but you may find yourself sleeping tenuous inches from the ceiling on a platform bed/desk combination. In that case, be prepared to bump your head most mornings. For the first part of freshman year, it's not uncommon to see students polarized into different social groups based on their residence hall. The University even stresses this division with a Dorm Wars competition during orientation week. For first-year students, pride in their dorm can be very important. As a freshman, you'll want to live in first-year housing, as it provides a social atmosphere among the most affable students. This means living in Morewood E-Tower, New House, Donner, or some of the all-freshman floors in Mudge.

B-

The College Prowler® Grade on
Campus Housing: B-

A high Campus Housing grade indicates that dorms are clean, well-maintained and spacious. Other determining factors include variety of dorms, proximity to classes and social atmosphere.

Off-Campus Housing

The Lowdown On...
Off-Campus Housing

Undergrads in Off-Campus Housing:
28%

Average Rent For:
Studio Apt.: $550 per month
1 BR Apt.: $700 per month
2 BR Apt.: $850 per month

Popular Areas:
Beeler Street
Squirrel Hill
Shadyside
Oakland

For Assistance Contact:
Community Housing Services
www.housing.cmu.edu/ CommunityHousing
(412) 268-4990
commhous@andrew.cmu.edu

Students Speak Out On...
Off-Campus Housing

> **"There are a lot of places close to campus, and rent is pretty cheap here. The places are pretty nice for student housing."**

Q "If you choose to leave campus housing after your freshman year, you should make sure you have a place to live for the rest of your time at CMU, because **getting back into campus housing is nearly impossible**. There are some decent apartments close to campus if you don't like dorm life."

Q "I would move out of a dorm after freshman year; **it's refreshing, and you can have a nice place**. Many students move into houses or apartments with friends. Rent is pretty cheap in Pittsburgh, so it's not hard to find a good place. Some people live as far as a fifteen-minute bus ride, but the buses are really good and come often, so it's not that bad."

Q "It is very convenient, and **very much worth it** to live off campus. You have to be careful where you choose to live, but the value is better and the community is less irritating."

Q "There is very convenient housing all over the place and around school. **It's much cheaper** than living in school dorms."

Q "**Commuting can be a pain**. Fraternities are essentially on campus, and are a much better option."

Q "It's very convenient, and I recommend it. Don't be one of those dorks that lives on campus in a dorm for his whole college career. **Get off campus ASAP**."

Q "**Off-campus housing is extremely convenient**. There are a lot of apartments and houses nearby for rent; there have to be, with so many students in the city. I live off campus, which is a beautiful 22-minute walk for me. It's safe also. Usually first-year undergraduate students are required to live on-campus. I prefer that because you get to meet some great people when you have to live with them."

Q "Off-campus housing is pretty easy to find. **There are houses everywhere**! It's just a question of finding one that's close. I prefer to stay close to campus, and it can be hard getting a reasonable apartment close to campus. If you find people to live with, you can get into a house and that makes things much nicer and definitely cheaper."

Q "There are a lot of houses really close to the school, but they will probably be somewhat more expensive than on-campus housing. On the other hand, you will get a lot more space, but you will also probably have to pay for things like utilities. If you live a little farther from campus, you can still take the bus to school, and housing might be cheaper than on campus. **You'll get a lot more space**. You might want a car if you do that, since you might have a garage and free parking."

Q "Off-campus housing is easy. **There are nice residential neighborhoods** with lots of apartments available. Since the University of Pittsburgh pretty much adjoins our campus, landlords know that they will always have students who are looking for places to live."

Q "**Campus housing is very expensive**. Eventually—probably my junior year—I will be moving off campus. There are a bunch of apartments you can rent out. Housing offers apartments off-campus, which you might get into if you don't send in your housing payments on time. They are nice apartments and they are quieter, but you can switch into the dorms after the first semester if you want to. I like the apartments because I feel I have a nice separation from the school."

Q "Off-campus housing is very convenient, and **all within walking distance**. If that's what you're going for (and I would), arrive earlier in the summer to get a place squared away. They do go quick. There are always people looking for roomies, though."

Q "Well, next year will be my second year living off campus. After living off campus, **I could never imagine living on campus**. But for the first year or two, on-campus living is definitely the way to go. I know that's how I met most of my friends. But with off-campus housing, we have an entire house to ourselves, there's parking, and you don't have to deal with resident assistants and all that school stuff. You gain more responsibility with monthly rent and bills, too. I would highly recommend living off campus the last two years."

The College Prowler Take On...
Off-Campus Housing

There's a large selection of houses and apartments to choose from in the nearby area. Most students love their off-campus residences, but the relationship between students and their houses is not without its pains. Having your own place is a great thing for a student, and dealing with things like paying bills, getting enough heat, trekking to campus, and even being wary of suspicious housemates is not enough to dampen the experience of having your own place. Students can find themselves spread out in Oakland, Shadyside, and Squirrel Hill, but most students renting houses end up living on nearby Beeler Street. The street itself is like a small community of CMU students living off campus. On the weekends, there's usually at least one party somewhere close by.

Finding off-campus space isn't much of a problem. The housing department makes it trouble-free to find and secure a location and provides students with information packets and many private listings only available to the CMU community. Unfortunately, you'll probably have to do at least ten minutes of walking to get to campus. This isn't so bad though, especially considering the impressive condition of many of the houses and apartments. If you can find an off-campus place that is well-maintained and set up so that you don't have to pay for utilities (Pittsburgh has freezing winters), the move from campus to a nearby apartment or house is definitely worth it. If you can find a bunch of friends to live with and drive down rent, think about moving off campus by at least your junior year. Be careful though! Students warn that campus housing can be a disaster if you don't check out the place before you choose to rent it.

A

The College Prowler® Grade on

Off-Campus Housing: A

A high grade in Off-Campus Housing indicates that apartments are of high quality, close to campus, affordable, and easy to secure.

Diversity

The Lowdown On...
Diversity

Native American:
1%

White:
53%

Asian American:
23%

International:
12%

African American:
5%

Unknown:
1%

Hispanic:
5%

Out-of-State:
67%

Most Popular Religions
There are a lot of Christian groups. Most religious activity takes place off campus.

Political Activity
Most students are politically and socially liberal. Though the campus has its share of protests, students are generally not outspoken about their political views. Many consider the student body to be somewhat apathetic.

Gay Pride
The campus is very accepting of its gay students and has on-campus student groups such as SoHo, CMUout, ALLIES, and SafeZone. However, like most of CMU's student body, the sizable gay community is relatively quiet.

Economic Status
CMU has students from diverse economic backgrounds, but most seem to have wealthy parents. Some students complain about all the "rich kids."

Minority Clubs
CMU's minority clubs are a noticeable social force on campus. The college offers a number of Asian and Indian clubs that throw parties and sponsor different events. There's also an African American fraternity, an Asian fraternity, and a Jewish fraternity.

Students Speak Out On...
Diversity

> **"I feel like it's really diverse. I hear at least three different languages other than English every day."**

Q "The **campus is more diverse than New York City**. There is a large Asian population, several Indians, and then a bunch of others. Although really diverse, people often stick with their own kind. Many come straight off the boats, so they feel like they need to stay with people like themselves."

Q "The campus is very diverse. This is **one area where the school really shines**. Kids come from the U.S., Canada, Mexico, Asia, Europe, Africa . . . everywhere. There are all sorts of people with all sorts of interests. Unfortunately, I only get along with about ten or fifteen of them."

Q "I think the campus is **quite diverse**. The student population is, first of all, almost 25 percent Asian, and over 10 percent international (students from other countries). However, the male/female ratio is three to two or so; it's something like 70 percent male!"

Q "It's very diverse. I'm Asian, and I was born in Baltimore. My high school was 97 percent white, and here something like one-third is made up of 'minorities,' so it's very different. It's still nice, and **people are from all over the states and the world**. They all have different backgrounds; it's nice in that respect."

Q "There's an enormous amount of diversity. There's a large Asian and Indian student body, but **no racial tension**. It's a very comfortable environment in that respect. One of the things I love about CMU is that you meet people from every place imaginable."

Q "It's very diverse. A lot of people are **fresh off the boat from other countries**. There are kids from all across the United States. There are not many black people or Hispanics, but we have a lot of white, Chinese, Japanese, Indian, Korean, and Arab students. As in all colleges though, it's pretty segregated. The Asians stick with the Asians, the blacks with the blacks, the farm boys with the farm boys."

Q "The campus is very diverse, **maybe even too much**, in my opinion."

Q "There are lots of people from eastern countries, but **very few African Americans**."

Q "It's pretty diverse. **I'm white, and I feel like a minority**."

Q "There's next to **no African Americans**, and we've got lots of Asians. There are lots of cultural groups out there if you want them."

Q "Well, there is a large international community, especially from Asia. Sometimes they can be very **cliquey and close-minded**, but sometimes they add a little insight into other cultures."

Q "The diversity is quite good. There's a decent number of minorities and international students. **The male/female ratio could use some work, though**."

Q "I think it is very diverse, not only ethnically, but also in interests. Sometimes everyone is so focused on studying that it's difficult to take advantage of the diversity, but if you get involved in student activities, **you'll meet all sorts of people**."

Q "I'd say CMU has a lot of Asians and Americans, but **there are actually not that many blacks**. It's kind of different for me, and I guess it's not as great as I would like it to be."

The College Prowler Take On...
Diversity

Carnegie Mellon prides itself on its diversity. The opportunity students have to meet people of different races, religions, and backgrounds is something that has a phenomenal impact on student life. Campus diversity gives a worldly experience to the students of a school isolated deep within Western Pennsylvania. As students claim, it never really feels like any race on campus is a majority (even though whites outnumber other races). The ethnic whirlwind that is CMU can be a bit dizzying at times. Because of the school's unprecedented diversity in some areas, it's easy to forget that there are some groups that aren't fairly represented, namely females. Carnegie Mellon's piteous male/female ratio is a major detractor to prospective students (as well as a constant downer for some male students). It's also true that the campus does not have a sizable African American or Hispanic population, especially when compared to the high concentration of other minorities. That said, the mélange of students at CMU is like nothing else most students have ever experienced.

Except for the dearth of women, all different races, religions, classes, and, geographic regions can be found in abundance on campus. As a student, CMU's diverse environment is a way to further your education by learning about the differences among people. If you're eager to learn about other cultures, Carnegie Mellon can provide a fantastic real-world education.

A-

The College Prowler® Grade on

Diversity: A-

A high grade in Diversity indicates that ethnic minorities and international students have a notable presence on campus, and that students of different economic backgrounds, religious beliefs, and sexual preferences are well-represented.

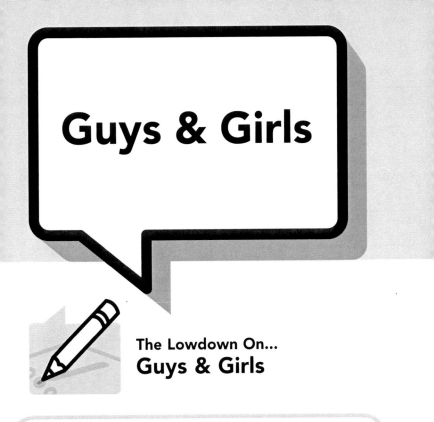

Guys & Girls

The Lowdown On...
Guys & Girls

Men Undergrads:
61%

Women Undergrads:
39%

Birth Control Available?
Yes. Female students who have had an exam with their home doctor or have an exam with Health Services can have their birth control prescriptions filled at health services for $10. Health Services offers all forms of birth control; pills, patches, and the shot. They also sell discounted condoms for 25 cents.

Hookups or Relationships
A lot of girls on campus are in relationships, but not always with CMU guys. There is a sizable pool of singles, however, and commitment-free hookups can be a common occurrence if you want them to be.

Social Scene

Initiating interaction on campus is one of the greatest social hurdles CMU students have to face. Once students find their niche, however, it's not that bad. Poor social interaction is a downside that many students expect when coming to a school filled with introverted and focused young adults (nerds). There is really no social hierarchy on campus, and you can usually find a social butterfly for every kid who's socially awkward. The biggest challenge here is getting people to mix with others beyond their majors, colleges, or clubs.

Best Place to Meet Guys/Girls

Students are so involved in their studies and other activities that it's not surprising for guys and girls to hit it off while studying in the dorms, taking notes in class, or working on extracurricular activities. For students who don't want their romantic life to be too scholastic, there are some good house parties most weekends where singles go in hopes of meeting a significant other. Going to clubs and bars is a good way to meet non-CMU students who are out to have a little fun.

Dress Code

This is not a preppy school. Yes, some students do dress sharp, but the number of students wearing AMD Processor shirts is usually greater than the number of students wearing A&F. Most students don't have time to think about how they're going to dress and just roll out of bed and go to class unkempt. When it's time to party, however, the guys clean up and the girls spend time getting ready. Anything goes here. This school has trench coats, capes, jeans, and Prada. You'll see your share of shorts in the middle of winter—even if it is thirty degrees out.

Important Note!

If you're looking to up your odds, you might have to wait to the end of the spring semester, when the number of "hotties" at CMU seems to flourish. This is the time when students trade their bulky coats for tank-tops and venture into the sun after months of being sealed in their dorm rooms and computer clusters. This is also the best time of the year to grab a blanket and go out to the middle of campus ("The Cut") in hopes of spotting some hot young women and studly young men tossing a football, listening to music, and maybe even having a few discrete drinks.

Did You Know?

Top Places to Find Hotties:

1. The Cut
2. The Frats
3. The Computer Clusters

Top Places to Hook Up:

1. Frats
2. The football field
3. Empty classrooms
4. Flagstaff
5. Off-campus parties

Students Speak Out On...
Guys & Girls

"I believe it was *Playboy* who ranked CMU as one of the top ten ugliest campuses, but if you manage to get into the drama department, you'll find many hotties awaiting your arrival."

"**Everyone's really smart**. I've never met so many socially inept people in my whole life. People are of average good looks in general, but it's tarnished by the fact that most students do not observe good hygiene."

"There are more guys than girls, so you think it'd be great for girls, but actually **people at CMU are really eclectic** and you may only be attracted to .0007 percent of the opposite sex. Come to CMU and see why. There's a saying on campus: 'Sex kills. Come to CMU and live forever.'"

"Ha! **The girls leave much to be desired**. I don't know what it is, but CMU attracts a wholly undesirable kind of girl. I am so unsexed and bitter that I didn't pick a school with a better girl-to-guy ratio. I have no idea how the guys are. I suspect they'd be a catch because they're going to be very financially secure someday."

"**People are so geeky here**. I've heard some science majors refer to having sex as 'knitting genes.'"

"If you are looking for someone to date, try the College of Fine Arts first, even though there are others. Plus, the University of Pittsburgh adjoins our campus; with around 30,000 students, there is something for everyone! Of course, we all know that **looks aren't important**."

Q "We're certainly **not the most attractive campus**, but it's not like there aren't any attractive people around. There's the University of Pittsburgh and a few other colleges around. The male-to-female-ratio is three to two, but we're a nerd school; what do you expect? When you get out of here and you're starting off at about fifty or sixty grand a year, it'll all be worth it."

Q "During my freshman year in the computer science department, **there were more guys named David than there were girls, period**. I wouldn't say that the majority of the girls are 'hot,' but there are plenty of good lookers if you know where to go. You are better off 'sightseeing' down the street at the University of Pittsburgh. Usually, a lot of females from area colleges come by the fraternities on the weekends."

Q "Supposedly, *Playboy* magazine once rated CMU as the **second ugliest campus in the country**, except for the College of Fine Arts (CFA). That's not really true, but there are lots of funny-looking people (which I think makes the school interesting). The part about the CFA is true, however. I don't know how it happens, but the fine arts students are usually always good looking. I don't want to say this just because I'm a drama student, but the truth is our profession and area of study relies heavily on looks because the faculty wants us to be marketable in the professional world. Since we want to be successful actors, part of that includes what we look like. This also applies to the musicians. In general, the students in CFA are either hot cute, interesting, or have a marketable look."

Q "We are right next to the University of Pittsburgh, so even though the actual campus population may be lacking in good looks, there are always **good-looking people right next door**. The bar and club scene can be pretty active, but I am a computer science major, so I rarely have time for that. Usually, I am more into independent parties, and since I already have a girlfriend, I don't need to go clubbing."

Q "A lot of **people tend to stick to their own**. We have a lot of Indian or other Asian people, and they tend to hang out with only other Indians or Asians. The social scene on campus can be pretty depressing. For the most part, you will probably want to shop at Pitt for chicks. There are a few 'hotties,' though, and if you're decent-looking where you live now, then your attractiveness multiplies by 10 here; most of the guys are tiny fat little nerds, and chicks don't go for that. A lot of the women aren't much better. There are some good looking ones, but the majority isn't. It's depressing."

Q "I don't check out guys, but **girls are usually not hot**. Actually, believe it or not, it depends on the weather. You see, when it's cold and perhaps snowy, girls wear way too much clothes. That just takes all the sexiness away. Once summer comes it's like, 'Hey, this school is starting to get better.' What's also cool about the sunny days is that a lot of people chill outside and sit on the grass, or play sports. That's cool."

Q "The saying on campus for guys is, 'The odds are good, but the goods are odd.' There are a lot of nerds, but the **guys are generally decent and really nice**. A lot of them sit in front of the computer playing games all day. I heard that *Playboy* chose our school as one of the ugliest schools for girls a couple of years ago. It's not that bad, though."

Q "You would think the guys would be hot considering the larger proportion of guys, but they're not. Well, I guess there are a few, but **they're most likely taken**. The guys that I made friends with are extremely nice. I haven't really met a jerk yet. The girls are girls, and it really depends on who you hang out with, I guess. I know I made a bunch of really good friends first semester, and now we're living together next year!"

Q "The guys are plentiful. You have a wide variety, from the jocks, to the antisocial computer nerds, to the artists, to everything. **The girls are becoming more plentiful**, and people are more attractive than the typical stereotype of CMU. Besides, both the boys and girls have strong money potential when they graduate."

Q "There are more guys than girls, so **girls have good odds**. However, there are a bunch of anti-social folks because they are always working on computers and engineering things."

Q "I heard once that this was actually **the second-ugliest campus in the country**. I don't believe this because of the lookers in the College of Fine Arts. The CFA kids are pretty hot, especially those in drama. This is one of the top drama schools in the country, and they want to produce talented people with a look that's marketable for TV, stage, and film. You find a CFA guy or girl, and you're golden!"

Q "**It's not that hot both ways**. There are lots of 'freaks and geeks,' including me. Attractive girls are in extremely short supply, but they have quite a choice due to the unbalanced male/female ratio."

The College Prowler Take On...
Guys & Girls

CMU students will unabashedly tell you that their campus is not an attractive one. It doesn't help the situation any that the cold weather forces guys and girls to stay bundled up in coats and jackets for most of the year. The lopsided male/female ratio is hard for both sexes, but especially for the guys. CFA students seem to be really proud of their looks. All the physical praise for CMU's artistic students isn't unfounded; most of them are pretty fine. Many of the students studying less technical fields are actually pretty normal-looking. There are some students, though, who aren't too concerned about their looks or hygiene, and this is one of the reasons that the school has gotten such a bad reputation as a place to find hot guys and girls.

Students aren't coming to CMU looking for hotties. Due to the great disparity in gender, most girls would think their chances of finding a man are pretty good at CMU. However, most girls on campus have had to find consolation in the saying, "The odds are good, but the goods are odd." The situation for guys at CMU isn't as bad as some would think either. When you've exhausted the limited pool of CMU ladies, you can always outsource your romantic interests to Pitt, where the women are in abundance. Nonetheless, this is not the school for exploratory sexual exploits, though some students, especially those in CFA, have been known to get a little wild.

The College Prowler® Grade on
Guys: C-

A high grade for Guys indicates that the male population on campus is attractive, smart, friendly, and engaging, and that the school has a decent ratio of guys to girls.

The College Prowler® Grade on
Girls: D+

A high grade for Girls not only implies that the women on campus are attractive, smart, friendly, and engaging, but also that there is a fair ratio of girls to guys.

Athletics

The Lowdown On...
Athletics

Athletic Division:
NCAA Division III

Conference:
UAA

School Mascot:
Tartan

Colors:
Scarlet and White

**Males Playing
Varsity Sports:**
259 (8%)

**Females Playing
Varsity Sports:**
104 (5%)

➜

Men's Varsity Sports:

Basketball
Cross-Country
Football
Golf
Soccer
Swimming
Tennis
Track

Women's Varsity Sports:

Basketball
Cheerleading
Cross Country
Soccer
Swimming
Tennis
Track
Volleyball

Club Sports:

Aussie Rules Football
Badminton
Baseball
Crew
Cycling
Explorers
Fencing
Ice-Hockey
Lacrosse
Softball (Women's)

(Club Sports, continued)

Squash
Ultimate Frisbee
Volleyball (Men's)
Water Polo
Wrestling

Intramurals:

Badminton
Basketball
Bowling
Call Pool
Chess
Darts
Euchre
Floor Hockey
Foosball
Football
Indoor Soccer
Kickball
Pinochle
Racquetball
Soccer
Softball
Spades
Table Tennis
Tennis
Ultimate Frisbee
Volleyball
Water Basketball
Water Polo

Fields
Gesling Stadium, Intramural (IM) Field

Getting Tickets
There's no need to get tickets to attend a CMU sporting event. Even at the most important football games, the bleachers are only spotted with spectators.

Most Popular Sports
On the varsity level, the football and soccer teams have the largest presence on campus, but that presence is still pretty small. All of the IM sports are very popular. Volleyball seems to have mass appeal across campus, and ultimate Frisbee and crew have their cult followings.

Overlooked Teams
The club baseball team has been trying to go varsity for a few years but has so far been unable to get the money from the University.

Best Place to Take a Walk
Schenley Park or Frick Park

Gyms/Facilities

Skibo Gym
Skibo Gym is the largest gym on campus, but due to its very poor condition, it's clearly not the best. Though the gym does boast an expansive free-weight collection, most of the weights are falling apart. The weight room is often too crowded on afternoons to accommodate the number of students looking to lift. The gym does feature several basketball courts, indoor tennis courts, all-purpose rooms, track equipment, and a fencing room. There's some cardio equipment, but half of that equipment is usually broken.

UC Gym

The UC Gym is a series of athletic facilities located within the University Center in the middle of campus. In addition to a small but well-kept weight-room, the gym also features an aerobics room (with classes taught regularly by faculty) and a cardio room. The most impressive features of the UC Gym are its popular basketball courts, five squash/racquetball courts, and a recreational swimming pool.

Outdoor Tennis Courts

These six beautiful outdoor courts are built into the ground and are lighted for nighttime play.

Students Speak Out On...
Athletics

> "What varsity sports? If you love sitting in the bleachers with your friends and cheering on the football team, Carnegie Mellon is not for you."

Q "Intramural (IM) sports are pretty popular. We've got many different sports and leagues **based on ability**."

Q "**Do we have sports on campus**? I'm just joking, but that's how most of the student body feels. We are not an athletic school, and it's rare to hear anything about our football team. You can start any IM sports team you want. You can even play 'gaming' (people playing online computer games against each other). It's quite competitive on Sunday afternoons."

Q "What? We play sports here? You mean the **chess team or the ping-pong club**, right?"

Q "**Varsity sports aren't very big**; we're Division III. I think IM, on the other hand, is huge. I'd say about 75 percent of the campus plays some sort of IM sport."

Q "**IM sports are huge on campus**. A good majority of the students play one of the IM sports. There are tons of them. Varsity sports aren't as big to watch compared to other schools."

Q "Do we have varsity sports? Seriously, sports like **track and crew have a pretty good showing**, but that isn't a reason to come here. IM sports are pretty huge if you can find a good group to enter them with."

Q "Sports are decent. We have a good football team, but **no one really watches them**. We are surprisingly good at a lot of stuff. IM is pretty big. I play just about everything on IM, and there are around fifty sports you can play. They go year-round, so if you want to play sports, you can."

Q "I wanted to try out for tennis, but didn't like the coach too much, so I didn't try out. **Intramurals are pretty big**. I imagine it's because most people want to devote most of their time to studying, so intramurals are convenient for them."

Q "Varsity sports aren't that big to people. A lot of **people are too into studying and work to support athletics**. I play football, but I had more people at my high school games. A lot of people play IM, though. They have a lot of sports, and a lot of people participate."

Q "IM is much bigger than varsity. **CMU is hardly a school for jocks**, but it is good for people that just want to have some fun. There's some nice competition. There's even a golf course basically on campus."

Q "Well, it's a Division III school. There's support for the varsity and club sports, but it's **not really an overwhelming spirit**."

Q "Varsity sports are doing really well. **I'm on the swim team, and we recently placed fourth in the nation**. I know a lot of athletes, and it's a great group to be in. Almost everyone I know is in at least one IM sport. There are a ton of them to join. I was in six, I think."

The College Prowler Take On...
Athletics

Varsity sports may feature competitive play, but their popularity falls short when compared to the enormous success of intramural sports on campus. Though neglected by students, Carnegie Mellon's Division III sports are still important to the athletes that play them. CMU competes against Emory, NYU, Wash. U, Case Western, and Brandeis in the University Athletic Association. The large number of students involved in IM sports is shocking to some, considering the school's un-athletic reputation. The Frisbee and crew club teams have a devoted following and provide a social atmosphere for their participants. Playing these sports is a fun and lighthearted way for most students to stay in shape in between studying.

Athletics events on campus are only important to the athletes involved in them. If you've always dreamed of coming to a college where you could cheer the football team to victory every weekend, you need to go down the street about half a mile to the University of Pittsburgh (or become a Steelers fan). The best way to experience the excitement and competition of sports is to create it yourself. Sign up for your own IM team, give it a crazy name, and when the referee calls you for a foul, curse him out like it's game seven of the NBA Finals.

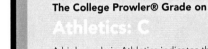

The College Prowler® Grade on

Athletics: C

A high grade in Athletics indicates that students have school spirit, that sports programs are respected, that games are well-attended, and that intramurals are a prominent part of student life.

Nightlife

The Lowdown On...
Nightlife

Club and Bar Prowler: Popular Nightlife Spots!

Club Crawler:

Déjà Vu Lounge

620 Penn Ave, Strip District

(412) 263-2877

www.dejavuloungepa.com

Déjà Vu is a nice place to relax and unwind during the evenings but can get pretty packed at night.

It's a lounge/club with different rooms that play a mix of techno and Top 40. Drinks are probably the most expensive in the city, but the dress code is not that strict. Many people go here first since there is no cover and then head down the block to Sanctuary later in the night. You must be 21 to get in, and IDs are not checked too hard.

Light Nightclub

1501 Smallman Street,
Boardwalk Complex,
Strip District

(412) 281-1585

Light makes up half of the infamous "Boardwalk" in the Strip District. You must be 21 to get into Light, and you must be dressed properly. They don't allow hats, throwbacks, tucked-in sweaters, doo-rags, or army wear. Parking is usually around $5 and is right outside of the club.

Margarita Mama's

1 East Carson Street,
Station Square

(800) 242-4842

Margarita Mama's is a two-area bar with a central bar, booths, and pool tables on one side, and another bar and big dance floor on the other. There are specials every night of the week, and Thursdays are popular college nights—a college ID gets you in for free.

The Matrix

1 Station Square Unit E7,
Station Square

(412) 261-2220

www.matrixpgh.com

Occupancy: 1,000

The Matrix combines four different rooms into one night club. Club Liquid plays Miami-style trance,

(The Matrix, continued)

Club Exit plays '80s dance hits, Club Goddess plays Top 40 music and corny old-school hip hop, and Club Velvet plays Latin music that is slightly old. The Matrix is a really nice club, and gets very packed, but they have a dress code. The best day to hit up the Matrix is without a doubt on Thursday.

Sanctuary

620 Penn Avenue,
Strip District

(412) 263-2877

Sanctuary is an upscale dance club that plays everything from 50 Cent to Madonna's "Like a Prayer." This club used to be a church, but they renovated it to make it really nice inside. Waitresses are dressed up as Catholic school girls. The people usually dress nicer here than in other clubs in Pittsburgh, and drinks are more expensive as well. Don't expect to find any drink specials or wild college kids here. There's a strict dress code, and you must be 21. Fridays and Saturdays are the best nights to go.

Tequila Willies

1501 Smallman Street,
Boardwalk Complex,
Strip District

(412) 281-1585

Occupancy: 600

TW's makes up the other half
of the "Boardwalk." Same
type of dress code as Light.
You pay one cover to get
into the Boardwalk and have
access to both Tequila Willies
and Light. You must be 21 to
get in and they scan IDs at
the door to make sure they
are real. The best night to
hit up Light and TW's is on
Wednesday.

Bar Prowler:

Mad Mex

370 Atwood St.,
Oakland

(412) 681-5656

The place to go for giant
margaritas and Mexican food.
Thanks to popular student
specials and happy hours, the
place is usually packed with
both Pitt and CMU kids. On
Fridays, many students come
here to start their weekend
at 4 p.m., when margaritas
and beers are half-off until 6
p.m. Things get even more
packed later in the evening.
From 9 p.m.–11 p.m., giant
margaritas are $6, and after
11 p.m., all food is half-off.
No one leaves here sober.

Panther Hollow Inn (PHI)

4611 Forbes Ave.,
Oakland/CMU

(412) 682-9999

This bar is a CMU tradition,
although you won't read
about it in any brochures.
Thursday nights at PHI are
packed with CMU students
taking advantage of $4
pitchers. It's a couple of steps
away from the dorms, right
on Forbes.

Peter's Pub

116 Oakland Ave.,
Oakland

(412) 681-7465

Peter's is a club on the
University of Pittsburgh's
campus located in the heart
of Oakland. It's a college
hangout with mostly Pitt
kids, but the CMU students
that know what's up come
here for fun. Thursday is
often the best night with $3
pitchers until 12 a.m. Monday
is great. You can dance to
the latest hip-hop upstairs
and rub shoulders with the
Pitt football and basketball
teams.

Pittsburgh Deli Company (PDC, The Deli)

728 Copeland St., Shadyside

(412) 682-DELI

PDC is another local bar within a short hike from campus. Located right off Walnut Street, this eclectic restaurant/bar offers live music throughout the week as well as half price food after 9 p.m. It's the closest thing Yuppie-style Shadyside has to a hippie bar.

Shady Grove

5500 Walnut St., Shadyside

(412) 697-0909

This is arguably one of the most popular places in Shadyside. Known for its trendy New York-style décor and a busy (and often loud) atmosphere, many students come here for beer specials as well as frozen margaritas and daiquiris. Right upstairs is the site of the Walnut Grill, a slightly more low-key room. Come up here to sip martinis. Stay downstairs if you want darts.

William Penn Tavern

739 Bellefonte Street, Shadyside

(412) 621-1000

The Tavern is a sports bar, with sports memoribilia decorating the walls. For entertainment, there are dart boards, foosball tables, video poker machines, and big screen TVs showing the day's most important sporting event. In the summer, you can enjoy your drinks and food at the outside tiki bar.

Other Places to Check Out:

Bar 11

Bash

Bossa Nova

Buffalo Blues

Chemistry

Club Havana

Dee's

Dowe's

Halo

Lava Lounge

Mario's

Pegasus Lounge

Shadyside Saloon

Shootz Café

Sports Rock

Tiki Bar

Touch

Student Favorites:

Déjà Vu Lounge

Matrix

Panther Hollow Inn (PHI)

Shady Grove

Tequila Willies

Useful Resources for Nightlife:

www.barsmart.com

www.pghnightlife.com

City Paper

Local Specialties:

Iron City

Rolling Rock

Yuengling

Primary Areas with Nightlife:

Oakland

Shadyside

South Side

Station Square

Strip District

The Waterfront

Cheapest Place to Get a Drink:

Panther Hollow Inn (PHI)

Favorite Drinking Games:

Beer Pong

Card Games

Century Club

Kings

Power Hour

Quarters

What to Do if You're Not 21

Club Zoo

1630 Smallman Street

Strip District

(412) 201-1100

Club Zoo is the hottest spot for under-21-year-olds to dance and party the weekend away. This club boasts 20,000 square feet, four levels, a VIP Room, and five bars. The bars serve free soft drinks, bottled watter, and energy drinks, as well as food and snacks. The high-tech lighting and sound systems keep underangers dancing on the bars and cages throughout the club.

Organization Parties

Many clubs at CMU will often rent out a restaurant or night club and throw private parties. These parties are usually a lot of fun and are thrown by groups such as Spirit, Architecture, Design, Asian Student Association, Korean Student Association, and the Indian Student Association. Look for these organizations to partner with similar ones at the University of Pittsburgh. These parties are usually a lot better.

Frats

See the Greek section!

Students Speak Out On...
Nightlife

{ **"Pittsburgh doesn't have the greatest nightlife, but they do have some kicking bars, especially on the South Side and in the Strip."**

Q "If you're coming to CMU for the parties and the bars, you may be thinking of Central Michigan University. That's the wrong CMU. During freshmen year, **frat parties are the big thing**. After that, you'll probably be going to a lot of house parties."

Q "Parties take place on the edges of campus and consist of **small, dull house parties which would be too tame for most people's parents**. Do not believe the hype— college is not like the movies. It's depressing how lame college kids can be. CMU is not the place to party, and Pitt is a little too rugged for your average CMU student. Get ready for four years of frustrating parties where your grandma is more hip than the average student. Clubs and bars are plentiful if you have a fake ID, which most people do. Work hard and play hard, I guess."

Q "Unlike New York, **there aren't very many bars and clubs for people under 21**. There are a few places that have eighteen-and-over nights on certain days of the week. However, Pittsburgh is a smaller and more family-oriented city, so late night spots aren't that prominent."

Q "Shootz, Mario's, and Peter's Pub are all good places to go. You really can't go wrong if you want to go to a bar and you're on the South Side. **The Strip has more clubs** and that kind of scene."

Q "I've been to one bar since I've been at CMU because I turned 21 a month ago. You have to be 21 to get into all bars (**Pennsylvania has very strict liquor laws**). There are plenty of them in Pittsburgh. Between Oakland, the South Side, the Strip District, and Downtown, there are many choices. I'm not into the club scene. The only ones that I know of are in Station Square."

Q "I haven't been to many bars or clubs, but my friends have. **There's also a gay club in downtown called Pegasus**. As far as bars go, there's a whole bunch. Just to let you know, there isn't anything in downtown except for some clubs, bars, and the symphony. It's like a ghost town at night, but there are things to do in Oakland, which is where CMU is."

Q "Off campus, **there are a bunch of bars in Oakland**. The typical CMU bar, where most CMU kids go, is PHI. They have some pretty good beer specials on certain days of the week. The South Side also has a ton of bars, but they're mostly full of Pitt and Duquesne students. The Strip District boasts the most clubs. Try the Matrix on Fridays, Sanctuary on Saturdays, and on Thursdays, go to PHI!"

Q "Those who are 21 and under can go to clubs in Oakland, down the block from CMU. You will find a mix of local Pittsburghers as well as CMU and Pitt students at the bars. **They can get pretty packed**, but they don't serve alcohol unless you have an ID. There is also Station Square, which is really nice and big, but that area requires a cab ride!"

Q "There is one bar in particular that CMU students go to because of its proximity to campus, and because it's inexpensive—PHI. **The club scene, if you have a good fake or are 21, is all right**. I'm from New Jersey, so it's nothing like New York City, but it's livable. For your first year, you'll probably do the frat scene, which is definitely fun as an underclassman, but it'll get old as the years go by."

"Oakland and Shadyside have some good bars close to campus. There is also the South Side a little farther away; its a few blocks of **nothing but bars and spots for college-age kids to hang out**. If you're looking for clubs, the Strip and Station Square are great spots with fancier dress codes."

The College Prowler Take On...
Nightlife

As students get older, their opportunities to experience good nightlife also grows. As freshmen, most students only venture so far as the frat quad. By sophomore year, most students know friends with houses, and there's the opportunity for a lot of off-campus parties. By junior and senior year, most students have turned 21 and are ready to go explore the Pittsburgh club scene. Students can hit this scene even earlier if they bring a fake ID with them to college. If CMU has an official bar, it's the always-packed PHI (Panther Hollow Inn) on Forbes Avenue. Students patronize the bar on all nights of the week, and it's not impossible to sneak in if you're under 21. The bar isn't the classiest place, and it's kind of cramped, but students keep coming back.

Until you hit 21, most of the area's nightclubs will be pretty much off-limits. The frat scene is always an option for girls interested in basement dancing and beer pong. Parties on campus are very segregated. At CMU, fraternities and sororities aren't the only groups that throw exclusive parties. Most of the time, if you go to a party, it is probably being thrown by some specific campus group or major. This is especially true for the students in the College of Fine Arts. It's just as common to hear someone talk about going to an art, architecture, design, or drama party as it is to hear someone talk about going to a frat party. There aren't a ton of house parties, but there are enough that students should have something to do every weekend.

The College Prowler® Grade on

Nightlife: B+

A high grade in Nightlife indicates that there are many bars and clubs in the area that are easily accessible and affordable. Other determining factors include the number of options for the under-21 crowd and the prevalence of house parties.

Greek Life

The Lowdown On...
Greek Life

Number of Fraternities:
12

Undergrad Men in Fraternities:
15%

Number of Sororities:
5

Undergrad Women in Sororities:
11%

→

Fraternities on Campus:

Alpha Epsilon Phi
Beta Theta Phi
Delta Upsilon
Kappa Delta Rho
Kappa Sigma
Pi Kappa Alpha
Pi Kappa Theta
Sigma Alpha Epsilon
Sigma Phi Epsilon
Sigma Tau Gamma
Sigma Nu
Theta Xi

Sororities on Campus:

Delta Delta Delta
Delta Gamma
Kappa Alpha Theta
Kappa Kappa Gamma
Zeta Psi Sigma

Other Greek Organizations:

Greek Council
Greek Peer Advisors
Interfraternity Council
Kappa Phi Lambda
Lambda Phi Epsilon
Order of Omega
Panhellenic Council
Pi Delta Psi

Did You Know?

Once a year, the fraternities and sororities participate in a **musical competition called Greek Sing**.

{ **"The only parties that are on campus are held at the frats. They usually have a pretty good turnout. If dancing in a sweaty, humid room isn't your thing, then you are out of luck."**

Q "I've been to some pretty fun frat parties. **The quality of frat guys depends very much on the fraternity**. Everyone I knew in Sigma Nu and Kappa Delta Roh were so nice. The Delta Tau Delta boys were jerks."

Q "I'd rather not spend my time talking about Greek life. **It's lame**."

Q "**Greek life is a simple excuse for frat boys to prey on inexperienced college girls** who just want to dance. If you desire sex and male friendship so bad that you will pay dues for it, then you were born to be in a frat. If you have any dignity and respect, a sense of individuality, and intelligence, you will stay away from a frat. The sorority girls are just lame and not hot."

Q "**Well, it's a nerd school**. Most of us are too busy doing work to party every weekend, but we do have our frats and whatnot. There is Carnival, though. It's a three-day weekend dedicated to partying that's hosted by the school; we deserve it."

Q "About 15 percent of the students are in the Greek system. **I wouldn't say that they dominate**, but there are always parties outside of the frats and over at Pitt. People who work hard usually like to party hard, as well, and that's my real take on that."

Q "Fraternity life has helped make me a good event programmer and leader. **It's really expanded my social horizons** and forced me to meet lots of wonderful people. Even though the guys that I first came to school with have mostly graduated, I have a huge network of friends that will probably remain strong throughout the years."

Q "I'm in a fraternity, Alpha Epsilon Pi. There are 12 fraternities and five sororities here. **They tend to dominate most of the social scene, especially for freshmen**. We party a lot on Fridays and Saturdays during the first few weeks. About 15 percent of the campus goes Greek."

Q "**It is a strong component but not an essential one**. You are never pressured to participate, but you are always welcome. Usually, the frats and sororities have weekend parties, but because academics here are so important, there are very rarely parties during the week. They are all usually involved with charitable organizations and service, and are a positive influence on the school."

Q "I came from the University of Florida, so **the Greek life sucks** in comparison. There is a fair number of frats and sororities here, but personally, I am not a frat guy, and I don't like a lot of the guys in them. They serve cheap beer, they smoke bad pot, and all they really want to do is get the virgins drunk and into bed. Some are okay, but they are mostly lame, and the sad part is they don't even know it. I get along just fine without the frats. They don't really dominate the social scene, but they certainly are a big part of it. There are other parties all the time besides theirs, so if you aren't into cheesy frats, you can find other stuff."

Q "**It's not that great, in my opinion**, although some are good. I'll tell you that it depends on which ones girls think are good—they'll go there."

Q "I would say it doesn't dominate the social scene, but then again, I'm not in a frat. Probably most people in frats would say it dominates the social scene, so I don't know. I've hung out in some of their parties, **they're okay**, but they're not the best. The hygiene really sucks sometimes."

Q "**Our Greek life is pretty small**. It definitely does not dominate the social scene because there are a lot of parties that are non-Greek oriented. From experience, frats are fun the first week of school; that's about it."

Q "There's a pretty visible Greek community, and **it's very popular on campus**. It's definitely not necessary to find a group of cool friends or be in the party scene, though. I'm not Greek, and I get along great."

Q "Have you ever seen *Animal House*? It's nothing like that. **The frats do not dominate**. There are plenty more things to do, but I guess it depends on whether you like going to frat parties or not. I'm not a huge fan, but sometimes they can be fun."

The College Prowler Take On...
Greek Life

Most outsiders are a little cautious of Greek life, but fraternity and sorority members share a proud allegiance to their organizations. The social scene at Carnegie Mellon is different from most other colleges. While it's true that frat parties make up a large percentage of the partying that takes place on and off campus, these events are never really big deals for non-Greek students. The influence that fraternities have on non-Greek students is a passive one, but the frat scene is popular for freshmen to explore even if they don't join. With the Morewood Gardens, New House, and Mudge dorms right next to the frat quad, freshmen have easy access to Panhellenic debauchery.

Students interested in the brotherhood or sisterhood that Greek life offers can find it at CMU. Orientation week is a good time to frequent frat parties and find out if going Greek is something you'd be interested in. Only around 15 percent of students go Greek, so there's really no pressure to join, and it does not signal the end of your social life at CMU. The sororities don't really throw any parties, but naturally, girls can go to whatever frat party they want, no questions asked. A number of Pitt girls actually come up to CMU because the frats are cleaner and safer than the ones at Pitt. Guys who aren't brothers may have a little more trouble getting in, but it's not impossible especially if you have friends who can get you on the guest list.

The College Prowler® Grade on

Greek Life: C+

A high grade in Greek Life indicates that sororities and fraternities are not only present, but also active on campus. Other determining factors include the variety of houses available and the respect the Greek community receives from the rest of the campus.

Drug Scene

The Lowdown On...
Drug Scene

Most Prevalent Drugs on Campus:

Adderall

Alcohol

Caffeine

Marijuana

Ritalin

Liquor-Related Referrals:
0

Liquor-Related Arrests:
38

Drug-Related Referrals:
0

Drug-Related Arrests:
1

Drug Counseling Programs

The Counseling and Student Development Center

(412) 268-2922

Services: alcohol assessment services, short-term counseling, support for children of alcoholics, alcohol-related literature

The Office of Student Affairs

(412) 268-2075

Services: educational programming for groups/organization, alcohol-related films and literature

Interfaith Counsel

(412) 621-8875

Services: religious pastoral counseling and pastoral care

Student Health Services

(412) 268-2157

Services: alcohol dependency assessments, evaluation of alcohol on physical well-being

The Health Educator, Nancy Schmidt

(412) 268-7888

Services: one-on-one counseling, educational programming for groups/organizations

Employee Assistance Program (LifeWorks)

(888) 267-8126

Services: alcohol assessment services, short-term counseling and referral services

Students Speak Out On...
Drug Scene

"Carnegie Mellon University doesn't have a lot of drugs. But if you're looking for drugs, the best place to go would probably be the frats."

 "I don't think that many kids at CMU use drugs, but the ones who do have enough money to hit the scene hard."

"You have to look hard for drugs. I haven't encountered people doing them. People drink, but drugs are not big. Go to Pitt for that kind of thing. They know about drugs."

"It's a pretty mild drug scene. If you're desperate enough for drugs then you'll find them."

"Same as anywhere, you can find it if you know the right people."

"Marijuana is probably the most widely-used drug, but I don't know much about it because I don't smoke. I don't like it. I know a few people who get a hold of stuff, but overall, substance abuse is relatively minor because people are smart here and know how to control what they do, whatever it is."

"My friends got cited for smoking pot and had to go to drug abuse meetings. The punishment was way too strict, and the police were jerks."

Q "I had an awful roommate in the beginning of the year. He did every drug imaginable. I think that a lot of colleges have their problems with drugs, but **there's not a big scene at CMU**."

Q "If you look hard enough, **you can find whatever your heart desires**. I'd start with the frats. I'm not saying we're all a bunch of druggies, but it is college, and everyone experiments on those cold winter nights. I mean, what else are you going to do? It's too cold to step outside."

Q "You can get it all at CMU if you know where to go. Drugs are bad, though, and you should stay away from them. I know tons of students who pretty much ruined their CMU education because of substance abuse. As far as peer pressure is concerned, you won't find that at CMU. **Drugs are usually prominent in the drama department**. I guess it's so that the actors and actresses can act better."

Q "It's there, but **it's not rampant**. The only drug use I personally encountered was people out in the dark smoking pot. You can certainly avoid it if you want to."

Q "You can get your hands on just about anything; **lots of people smoke weed**."

Q "I don't know; I don't hear people talking much about that. I think that if there are drugs, **people don't make such a big deal about it**, or maybe not many people do it. I don't think many people do it, but then again, I don't go around asking."

Q "I've heard a story about this guy who smoked pot all day without even going to school. He did it so much that **his room was always filled with smoke like a cave or something**. Oh, what happened to him? He got kicked out, of course."

The College Prowler Take On...
Drug Scene

You need to look pretty hard to find drug activity on campus. It always seems like students know of someone who's really into drugs, but no students themselves ever admit to descending into drug use. There is some noticeable use of softer drugs, however. Alcohol seems to be the drug of choice for most students and just about everyone knows that guy who sits in his room and smokes pot all day. Non-users feel very little pressure to indulge in drugs.

CMU has less drug use than your average high school. It's true that students sometimes freak out before a test and begin to fiend for caffeine. There are also rumors of Ritalin use, but like most drug use on campus, no one ever really admits to seeing it happen. Drugs are not a dominant force in CMU culture, even though it isn't that hard to obtain them.

The College Prowler® Grade on

Drug Scene: B

A high grade in the Drug Scene indicates that drugs are not a noticeable part of campus life; drug use is not visible, and no pressure to use them seems to exist.

Campus Strictness

The Lowdown On...
Campus Strictness

What Are You Most Likely to Get Caught Doing on Campus?

- Drinking underage
- Public urination or indecency
- Parking illegally
- Making too much noise in your dorm
- Downloading copyrighted materials
- Sending unsolicited e-mail (spam)
- Bringing food or drink in a cluster
- Running around on roof tops of buildings
- Having candles and incense sticks in your dorm
- Running stop signs
- Streaking on the field
- Not having a wristband for the gyms

Students Speak Out On...
Campus Strictness

> **"Your dorm room is your sanctuary. You can pretty much do whatever you want in there, and it's your own business. Campus police only get involved when your neighbors start complaining."**

Q "If you get caught with alcohol and are underage, **you will be cited**. But that is the case with almost anywhere you go. Drugs are not tolerated, either."

Q "**The police are very hardcore about drugs**, but not drinking. I've walked past CMU police drunk and carried people who have been passed out, and they just looked the other way."

Q "The campus police have this great policy; you have immunity if you're caught drunk as long as you're helping the other person you are with. Plus, **the school is really light on substance abuse penalties and so on**. Although the drug scene barely exists, it has plenty of room to thrive."

Q "Usually, if you have a 'drug-related emergency,' campus police will **get you to a hospital without asking any questions**."

Q "I think that the **campus police are not that strict about drugs**. Most people don't smoke in any buildings because it's not allowed and they abide by the rules, but with drinking, they aren't too strict, unless it's underage."

Q "**Don't get caught if you are underage**. They really are concerned about your safety, so if you are hurting, they will take you to the hospital and not get all on your case. But really, don't get caught."

Q "I'm not very sure about drugs, although I don't think they're allowed. I forgot because **it's rare to find drug problems** . . . maybe that's just what I think. Drinking is completely prohibited unless you are over the age of 21. There have been about five cases of problems involving alcohol consumption on my dorm floor alone, but I'm sure that there is much more illegal drinking going on everywhere on campus, not that campus police will be able to catch it all—unless there's a rat on the floor willing to report every illegal behavior he sees."

Q "**The police don't bother any parties beyond warnings about noise**, and even those are rare. They also aren't allowed to enter the fraternities on campus for no reason, so that's nice. If you're caught for anything, I don't think they'll press any real charges; everything's internal. Plenty of people smoke around campus and don't get caught. As long as you're not stupid, you're fine."

Q "They're not as strict as one would think. There is some kind of amnesty thing they have that if students call for help for themselves or their friends because of intoxication, they don't get charged. People sometimes get internal citations for disorderly conduct due to drinking, but I don't know anyone who has been arrested for underage drinking, just reprimanded. I think they are strict with drugs, but I think **some are considered worse than others**. I did have a friend who spent a night in jail for marijuana possession, but I don't think he was caught on campus. A fraternity got in trouble for drug use or possession of some kind, and their house was taken away for a year."

Q "The cops are cool with lots of things, as long as you're not obnoxious about it. **They'll stand outside of the frats on weekends** when parties are going on and talk to people. They just want to make sure people are okay and get home safely."

Q "CMU has an agreement with Pittsburgh police. Basically, let's say that you're out one night and your friend gets really trashed. CMU makes it possible for students to call campus police without any fear of getting into major trouble. **The most that can happen to you is that you will get a fine**. CMU does this just to ensure safety."

Q "They can be strict, but for the most part, **they turn a blind eye** unless someone complains. There are frat parties on campus and they aren't raided unless the police have reason to believe something is going on."

Q "You aren't supposed to drink in campus housing if you're underage, and drugs, of course, are illegal. **I know that people still do that stuff and get away with it**, but not always. Usually, underage drinking is caught at the fraternities, and the frats are the ones that usually get in trouble."

The College Prowler Take On...
Campus Strictness

The students say it best! The campus police really care about their safety. Students involved in drinking on and around campus never have a reason to be paranoid of getting a citation, unless they're acting really stupid. Close your dorm room door, and you and your friends can get plastered and bounce off the walls all night. As long as things are kept quiet and no one sees anything, there won't be any problems from the authorities. The police are here to protect students, not to bust them.

The campus realizes that most CMU students are mature and lets them enjoy their freedom. The drug and party scenes aren't too large, and they never really get out of control, so the police don't have much to worry about in the first place. Even though students don't have much to fear from authorities, they shouldn't try to test their patience either.

The College Prowler® Grade on
Campus
Strictness: A-

A high Campus Strictness grade implies an overall lenient atmosphere; police and RAs are fairly tolerant, and the administration's rules are flexible.

Parking

The Lowdown On...
Parking

Approximate Parking Permit Cost:
$840–$1,620 per year

Common Parking Tickets:
Expired Meter: $30
No Parking Zone: $40
Fire Lane: $100
Handicapped Zone: $200

CMU Parking Services:
(412) 268-2052
parking@andrew.cmu.edu
www.cmu.edu/ba/parking

Student Parking Lot?
Yes

Freshmen Allowed to Park?
No

Parking Permits

Faculty and grad students get priority selection for parking permits. It's very rare for undergrads to obtain a parking permit. Due to the overwhelming demand, you must apply for a parking permit and get put in the lottery drawing to obtain a spot.

Did You Know?

Best Places to Find a Parking Spot

- The meters in Morewood parking lot
- The loading zone on Tech Street (keep your blinkers on!)
- The hill next to Beta (Devonshire)
- Most places after 6 p.m. (parking lots begin opening up between 5 p.m. and 8 p.m.)

Good Luck Getting a Parking Spot Here!

- Margaret Morrison Street

The Boot!

If you accumulate three or more parking tickets, you'd better watch out! Your car will get a nice, bright orange lock on your wheel.

Students Speak Out On...
Parking

"Parking here is tough; it's a relatively urban campus and all teachers who commute also need spots. Parking gets easier as the day goes on; it generally costs money until 6 p.m., after which it is free."

"**There is very little parking on campus**. If you are lucky enough to get a parking permit, you have to pay between $800 and $1,200 per year for it. You are better off just riding the bus."

"They only have one parking garage that's too small, and it costs, like, a million dollars a year to park there. Most of the people I know who have cars **can't afford to drive** them to school."

"They really don't advise you to bring a car to school. It's a pretty bad situation. **Don't bring a car**! If you need to, you can apply for a campus parking pass, but good luck getting one. If you live off campus, you can apply for a city parking permit and park in specific zones. Bring a bike! It's free, you get exercise, and you can park it anywhere; there are bike racks all over. Plus, it will allow you to explore the city in places that the bus can't take you, and that are too far to walk to."

"Parking? Where? I think last year I must have gotten about ten tickets for parking, and my car has been towed once. In other words, **parking on campus is a pain**."

Q "Parking is strict. It is difficult to park on campus, and permits are super-expensive. I would say **don't have a car during your first year**. Throughout the residential areas in Pittsburgh, it's permit parking; some people buy permits from people so that they can park on one of the streets near campus. The permits for residents are only $20, but since they are in high demand, people have sold them for over $400."

Q "We get **free bus transportation** anywhere in the city with our student ID cards, so a car is not really necessary. I didn't have one my first two years here. I finally brought one this year, but I don't use it that often—just for going to the grocery store or driving home to Indianapolis for breaks. I've been here for four weeks and have not even used half a tank of gas!"

Q "Parking on campus sucks. **Let me reiterate: it's terrible**. There is little parking, and it's anywhere from $500 to $2,000 to get a parking pass. I live just off campus where there is street parking for $20 if you live in the area. If you live on campus, I do not suggest bringing a car, because they do ticket, and the fines add up."

Q "If you have a car, you usually have to pay monthly or yearly in order to get parking space, and it's pretty expensive. **There's not much need to have a car,** though, because on-campus housing (which is enforced for the first year) is really close to school and things aren't usually so far. The tuition includes a bus sticker, which lets you ride the bus for free inside Pittsburgh. If you can afford a car (and parking), and aren't afraid of driving it in the snow, then bring a car."

The College Prowler Take On...
Parking

Parking for students is not convenient, and bringing a car is not necessary. To get a campus parking permit, you'll have to be chosen in a lottery, and even then, you'll have to fork over a lot of money to end up parking a car you probably won't need to use all that much. Students also have trouble parking on the city streets surrounding campus, as spots are rarely available, but those renting a house have the option to purchase a city parking permit for about $20. This works out well, since the only students who really need cars are the ones who would use them to commute to campus. Freshmen can't have cars on campus, so it's not really an issue for first-year students.

Due to all the parking problems, having a car on campus is more of a burden than anything else. Most students enjoy walking around campus. Fortunately, there's no pressure to bring a car so if you don't have the nicest whip, don't worry. You can just leave that '88 Mercury Tracer at home.

D-

The College Prowler® Grade on

Parking: D-

A high grade in this section indicates that parking is both available and affordable, and that parking enforcement isn't overly severe.

Transportation

The Lowdown On...
Transportation

Ways to Get Around Town:

On Campus
CMU Shuttle Service
6:30 a.m.–6:30 p.m.
(412) 268-7433

CMU Escort
6:30 p.m.–2:30 a.m., after
2:30 a.m. by request
(412) 268-2323

Public Transportation
Port Authority Transit (PAT)
(412) 442-2000
Pick up bus schedules
from the University Center
Information Desk.

Taxi Cabs
People's Cab Co.
(412) 441-5343
Yellow Cab Co.
(412) 321-8100

Car Rentals

Alamo
(412) 472-5060
(800) 327-9633
www.alamo.com
Avis
(412) 472-5200
(800) 831-2847
www.avis.com
Budget
(412) 472-5252
(800) 527-0700
www.budget.com
Dollar
(412) 472-5100
(800) 800-4000
www.dollar.com
Enterprise
(412) 472-3490
(800) 736-8222
www.enterprise.com
Hertz
(412) 472-5955
(800) 654-3131
www.hertz.com
National
(412) 472-5094
(800) 227-7368
www.nationalcar.com

Best Ways to Get Around Town

Weasel a friend into a ride

Pittsburgh city buses—they are free, just bring your ID

A bike

A mean set of sneakers

Ways to Get Out of Town:

Airlines Serving Pittsburgh

American Airlines
(800) 433-7300
www.americanairlines.com
Continental
(800) 523-3273
www.continental.com
Delta
(800) 221-1212
www.delta-air.com
Northwest
(800) 225-2525
www.nwa.com
Southwest
(800) 435-9792
www.southwest.com
TWA
(800) 221-2000
www.twa.com
United
(800) 241-6522
www.united.com
US Airways
(800) 428-4322
www.usairways.com

Airport

Pittsburgh International Airport

(412) 472-3525

The Pittsburgh International Airport is 22 miles and approximately 30 minutes driving time from CMU.

How to Get to the Airport

Airlines Transportation Company Inc.

(412) 471-8900

Airport Flyer

Port Authority Transit's 28X Airport Shuttle

(412) 442-2000

The bus stops in front of Carnegie Mellon, and the trip takes about forty minutes. Free with student ID.

A cab ride to the airport costs $35.

Greyhound

Pittsburgh Greyhound Trailways Bus Terminal

(3 miles from campus)

990 Second Ave.

Pittsburgh, PA 15222

(412) 392-6513

(800) 231-2222

www.greyhound.com

Amtrak

Pittsburgh Amtrak Train Station

(4 miles from campus)

1100 Liberty Ave.

Pittsburgh, PA 15222

(412) 471-6172

(800) 872-7245.

www.amtrak.com

Travel Agents

Forbes Travel

5835 Forbes Ave., Squirrel Hill

(412) 521-7300

STA Travel

118 Meyran Ave., Oakland

(412) 683-1881

World-Wise Travel

3039 West Liberty Ave., Dormont

(412) 531-5555

Students Speak Out On...
Transportation

{ **"I feel like the transportation situation is pretty good. You can't really get from neighborhood to neighborhood, though. The transportation system only gets you around within different neighborhoods."**

Q "All CMU students get a sticker on their ID card that allows them to **ride the bus for free**. You can get anywhere you want on the buses and they come pretty often."

Q **"The buses are really great**! You can go just about anywhere via bus. You get a free Pittsburgh bus pass with your $36,000 tuition! That's really nice of them! A fun game to play on a Sunday is 'how far can you get in the city via the buses?' Try it sometime if you don't have work, but that'll never happen."

Q "Public transportation is real spotty. The buses go almost anywhere, but you never know what time they'll show up or how often. **Meet your feet**—your new favorite form of public transportation."

Q **"Buses are awesome, and they're free with your student ID**, so you can get anywhere in Pittsburgh and the surrounding neighborhoods."

Q "The bus system **takes you everywhere**—the mall, the suburbs, the airport, downtown—and there are several bus stops on campus."

Q "Public transportation—mainly the bus system—is great because **it goes everywhere and is free**! If you ever need to fly anywhere, the airport here is one of the best in the country! You can even catch a bus to and from the airport for free."

Q "Public transportation is great. **It's better than the shuttle bus that the campus provides**. You can ride as many times as you'd like as long as you have your ID."

Q "**You can't catch a cab by flagging them down**, but you can call them up and hope they'll arrive on time. Buses are easy to catch during the day. I say get a car, a fast one!"

Q "It can take you where you need to go; **you just need to know the schedule**. You pay for it as part of your student fees, anyway, so you might as well use it."

Q "I'm very impressed with the bus system. If you know the right buses, **you can really get around**."

Q "It's very convenient. CMU gives you stickers for access to the buses and as many rides as you can think of. **Buses are a pain sometimes, because they're often late**, but there are no major problems. You can get basically anywhere with them with some patience."

Q "**Pittsburgh transportation sucks**. The buses are always late and the way you pay is ridiculous. It's either 'pay enter' or 'pay leave.' I think it depends on what the driver wants, so it's a bit confusing."

The College Prowler Take On...
Transportation

Public transportation is the only way to travel for most students. Every student gets free access to the bus system, and most students take full advantage of this. Pittsburgh, as a city, is spread out among a number of distant areas. To get to most of these places, you'll need to take the bus, especially since driving can get a little confusing. Though it sometimes can be a pain to wait 50 minutes for a bus that doesn't seem like it's ever going to come, off-campus life would be crippled without the bus system.

It only takes a few weeks to learn the bus system, and once you've familiarized yourself with it, you're golden. Your CMU bus pass is your key to exploring all areas of the city. The PAT buses are some of the cleanest and safest around.

B+

The College Prowler® Grade on

Transportation: B+

A high grade for Transportation indicates that campus buses, public buses, cabs and rental cars are readily available and affordable. Other determining factors include proximity to an airport and the necessity of transportation.

Weather

The Lowdown On...
Weather

Average Temperature:

Fall:	53 °F
Winter:	30 °F
Spring:	50 °F
Summer:	71 °F

Average Precipitation:

Fall:	2.83 in.
Winter:	2.64 in.
Spring:	3.33 in.
Summer:	3.82 in.

Students Speak Out On...
Weather

> **"The weather is unpredictable at best. It's even freezing at the end of May! I like the weather, though, because it always keeps you on your toes. I'd be bored in a place where it never changed."**

Q "I can't stand the weather in Pittsburgh. I mean, there are some beautiful days, but then **some really crappy ones**. There is a lot of rain. We often have overcast skies, and it gets pretty cold. That's one bad thing, oh well! Mother Nature, what can one do?"

Q "Pittsburgh weather is . . . flaky. **It rains a lot in the spring** and fall, and it snows a lot in the winter. The winter can get really cold, so bring your long johns. The late spring is a great time to be on campus, though. The sunshine and warm weather brings students out of their rooms and into the Cut for some seriously-needed tanning."

Q **"The weather is freezing, miserable, and inhospitable**. You sometimes feel like God wants you to die in this freezing, hellish wasteland."

Q "It's pretty overcast most of the time. You'll get some sunny days, and you'll get some freezing cold days, but **bring a raincoat**. If you're from warm weather, you'd better be prepared for a frigid winter. Bring warm clothes. You'll live in hooded sweatshirts and comfy pants. People don't dress up for class; people wear whatever they want. Fashion isn't big, academics are."

Q "Weather sucks. It's freezing cold in the winter and blazing hot in the summer. **The seasons are all messed up**; they switch around all the time. It rains so much, and it's overcast most of the time. The bad weather makes Pittsburgh a much more depressing city than it would otherwise be. Then again, what did you expect from a city that sits inside a giant ditch?"

Q "Pittsburgh weather changes a lot! One day it will be 50 degrees, and the next it might be 90. **It rains often**, and the winter can be cold and snowy. I like it because it changes so much. One of my classmates is from Hawaii, where it is always 80 degrees and sunny. He loves it that the seasons change! I would say it is not too much different from New York City; we are only about seven hours away."

Q "The weather sucks. **I come from Florida, so I think it's horrid**. It was really hot in the summer, but right now it's beautiful because it's not too hot and it's not really cold. But, once winter hits, its winter. I mean, I have never lived in snow, so I think it sucks, but I can't really compare it to anything. It doesn't snow, like, eight inches, but it snows sometimes, and it gets kind of cold."

Q "**Weather is strangely unpredictable**. It may seem sunny in the morning, and it may suddenly start snowing in the evening. It may look fine during the day, and it may rain at night all of a sudden. I don't like the weather here at all. That's why I like to stay in my room most of the time."

Q "Most people think of Pittsburgh as a rainy, dreary city; but that is just the stereotype. It's hot in August and September. In October and November, it cools down. It's cold in December and snowy into January. **Springtime is nice; it's the best time of year in Pittsburgh**."

The College Prowler Take On...
Weather

In Pittsburgh, the blue sky is often obscured by gray clouds. On clear days, however, the town is like an entirely different place—people are cheery and the school's population almost seems to double. Students often complain about the weather. If the climate was nicer, maybe most students wouldn't always be holed up doing work.

One of the first jokes you'll probably hear about Pittsburgh will be about the weather. It's rare that you'll have a day where the blue sky is not obscured by gray clouds. Rain is a constant year round, and the snow was pretty bad last winter. In the summer, Pittsburgh gets really humid, and everyone does what they can to stay cool. When you come to campus in the fall, wear shorts and a T-shirt, but make sure to pack winter clothes; the weather gets very cold, very fast. Bringing some snow boots wouldn't be a bad idea, either.

The College Prowler® Grade on

Weather: C-

A high Weather grade designates that temperatures are mild and rarely reach extremes, that the campus tends to be sunny rather than rainy, and that weather is fairly consistent rather than unpredictable.

Report Card Summary

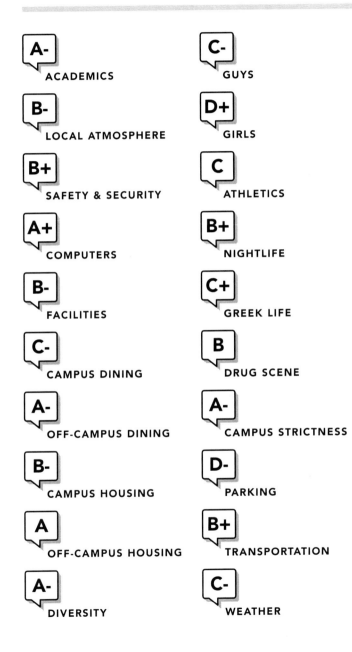

A- ACADEMICS

B- LOCAL ATMOSPHERE

B+ SAFETY & SECURITY

A+ COMPUTERS

B- FACILITIES

C- CAMPUS DINING

A- OFF-CAMPUS DINING

B- CAMPUS HOUSING

A OFF-CAMPUS HOUSING

A- DIVERSITY

C- GUYS

D+ GIRLS

C ATHLETICS

B+ NIGHTLIFE

C+ GREEK LIFE

B DRUG SCENE

A- CAMPUS STRICTNESS

D- PARKING

B+ TRANSPORTATION

C- WEATHER

Overall Experience

Students Speak Out On...
Overall Experience

"I like CMU a lot, but I wish it were in a different location. Pittsburgh weather can get you down sometimes, but luckily, you get twelve free sessions per year with a psychologist."

Q "I don't wish I were anywhere else. **CMU has a ton of really interesting people**. Students are racially diverse, live diverse lifestyles, and think different thoughts."

Q "It's not my type of place, because I'm more of a partier than most people. **I was more popular in high school than most people here**. I think a lot of people are into studying, but the fraternity I am in does plenty of partying, so I manage. To be honest, if the school wasn't so good for an education, I would be somewhere else."

Q "**Pittsburgh grows on you**, and then you realize that it is a really cool place. Don't expect it to be like other cities such as New York or Philly, because it's not. While those cities have a hot downtown, Pittsburgh, because of its history, doesn't have a great downtown scene, but it has incredible neighborhoods all over the place. Get to them all and check them out; there is some great stuff going on in there."

Q "I went to a larger university first and then transferred to CMU. **I like the small-school atmosphere**. You'll never be in a thousand-person lecture, and you'll always be able to get in touch with your professor or a TA. It's the kind of school that if you are ambitious and want to do something, you can do it. From starting a club to bringing a concert or event to campus, CMU is the kind of place that appreciates diversity and unique students and events."

Q "I wanted to transfer to Pitt my freshman year because I didn't think I was smart enough and I didn't really fit in with the competitive, nerdy people. That ended quickly, because I was too lazy to apply to Pitt. I can't see myself being anywhere else now. **You couldn't pay me to go to another school**. I'm practically obsessed with CMU now. You've got to love it for what it is. Tartan pride!"

Q "**This school is not for everybody**. CMU is a good institution that requires a lot of patience when dealing with the social scene and academic community. People here are weird. The campus is split into many subgroups of interests and studies. Do not believe what the school tells you about interdisciplinary studies; It's a crock! If I had to do it over again, I would go to a state school with a good media arts department. If you were a fairly social person in high school and enjoy going to parties and interacting with interesting and stimulating people, don't come to CMU. If you never took your head out of the books and now want a school that will accept you for being all the dork you can be, welcome home."

Q "I love CMU. Sure, there are minor things that I may dislike from time to time—things that you will find at any school—but after coming here, I cannot imagine going to any other school. This was the school for me because of the intense program. **This is not the place for everyone**, though. It's difficult to come here without having a sense of what you want to study. Everyone here in every academic program is highly focused. I'd say most students are very hardworking and really care. That's why it is such a good place for me; students are enthusiastic about their education. I really think this school is a great place, but you probably won't know for sure until you get here. I surely didn't."

Q "Here's the deal: If you are serious about education and you are serious about getting somewhere, then this place will help you do it. **This is not a big party school**. If you just want to mess around and party and get laid all the time, go somewhere else."

Q "**Job-wise, you can't do better than here**. It's a very good school, and there are a lot of opportunities. I'm not kidding about that; it's a great academic institution, but you have to be serious about it. You will work harder than you've ever worked before. I coasted through high school, but I'm majoring in cognitive science and computer science now, and it kicks my butt. As long as you are prepared to do the work, then you will have a great experience; everything else just sort of falls into place."

Q "I wanted to transfer to NYU for sophomore year, but as the semester went by, I met a lot of people, and they really made my experience at CMU a good one. Another friend wanted to leave initially, but now she absolutely loves it. Honestly, **I really enjoyed my freshman year**."

Q "It's a lot of work, that's for sure. I would definitely say that we get a lot more work than most Ivy schools, from what I've heard. If you're at CMU, and you're majoring in something that we're not known for, then I would definitely go elsewhere. If you're coming here for computers or engineering, and maybe business, then **the opportunities are endless**. I would never change schools for anything. Then again, I'm someone who would be comfortable anywhere. But, if you do come to CMU for any of those majors, be prepared to work your butt off. I believe CMU has a lot of weird people, but that's just because you're surrounded by people who are doing truly amazing things. I'm always impressed by my peers and I'm always proud of my school, but the social thing is not one of our strong points. You can get by, but it's definitely not one of our strengths."

Q "Here's a very important piece of advice: **Do not let first semester get you all worked up**. I think everyone has trouble adjusting. I was really considering leaving and going somewhere else, but that's not the case anymore. I expected all these things to happen when I got here and they didn't. Why they didn't happen was basically because I was living in a dream world. You just need to get adjusted, and that's the most difficult part. Also, when you're at orientation, be outgoing and meet as many people as you can! It's fun, it's hard, but you'll meet a lot of interesting people; trust me. Overall, I'm glad that I'm at CMU."

Q "I can't imagine being anywhere else. I actually just graduated, and I'm sticking around for the summer because I'm not ready to leave. I know I'll be back to visit, as well. I think **the school is so darn cool because of the diversity, and its strength in both the arts and sciences**. Not only is it one of the best computer science schools, but it's also one of the best drama schools (not to mention other majors, but those two are such opposites). I can't think of any other highly-ranked school that is so strong in such differing areas of study."

The College Prowler Take On...
Overall Experience

In appraising CMU, most students are appreciative of the fantastic education they're receiving and the one-of-a-kind experience that the campus offers. At CMU, students have an unprecedented opportunity to explore their fields of study. Sometimes it's hard for students to see all opportunities that Carnegie Mellon gives them. Students who are unhappy with their experience are often frustrated with the sub-par social situation or the massive amount of work.

No matter how fed up students get with the amount of work, the social scene, or the bad weather, students are often glad they came to CMU when they think about the unique experience the school has given them. The academic opportunities you will receive at CMU are astounding, and everyone on campus is truly dedicated to learning. Though the time spent at CMU may not fulfill some students' hopes of living a wild youth, the years spent at Carnegie Mellon can be just as exciting in some ways. It's different. And for people who don't want the same college experience as everyone else, it can be exciting.

The Inside Scoop

The Lowdown On...
The Inside Scoop

Carnegie Mellon Slang:

Know the slang, know the school. The following is a list of things you really need to know before coming to CMU. The more of these words you know, the better off you'll be.

Big Blue – Donner Residence Hall.

The Black Chairs – The black leather chairs in the middle of the UC where people meet; also known as the Airport Lounge.

Cat Man – Cathedral Mansions; campus-leased student housing apartments.

C-Cons – The computer lab assistants.

CFA – College of Fine Arts; Can't Fu***n' Add.

Cluster – A computer lab.

CS – Computer Science; Can't Score; Classes Suck.

CSW – Computer Skills Workshop.

The Cut – Carnegie Mellon's central lawn.

DA – Desk Attendant.

The Donner Ditch – An area behind Donner Hall. The site of numerous BBQs.

➜

The Dungeon – The basement of Donner Hall.

The Fence – Fence in the middle of campus that gets painted by students for tradition.

Fingering – A UNIX command to find information on a system user.

Flagstaff – A grassy hill behind Hunt Library and Baker Hall; part of Schenley Park.

H&SS – Humanities & Social Science; High School Studies; Hot, Sexy, & Stupid; H & Less Stress.

The Hub – Enrollment offices in the basement of Warner Hall. Pay your tuition here.

Moonlight – The Asian food truck.

P.H.I. or PHI BAR – Panther Hollow Inn, a popular bar right off campus.

The Mall – The grassy space between Baker, Hamerschlag, Wean, and Doherty Halls.

Maggie Mo – Nickname for Margaret Morrison, a building on campus.

MINI 1 & MINI 2 – One semester can be divided into two mini sessions. A few classes are offered in this shorter format.

MISC. MARKET – An online bulletin board where students post random messages and sell things.

The New Gym – The workout facility at the University Center.

The O – The Original Hot Dog Shop.

The Old Gym – Skibo Gym.

OLR – Online Registration.

The Quad – Where the fraternities are located.

Schlag – Hamerschlag Hall; a dorm.

Sree's – The Indian guy that sells food out of his truck.

The Trucks – Food trucks on Tech Street.

The UC – The University Center. This is the main student center on campus.

Things I Wish I Knew Before Coming to Carnegie Mellon

- Get on the smallest meal plan possible.

- Go to the frats during Orientation Week.

- Don't skip "Playfair" during Orientation.

- Don't buy the bed sheets and linens from the school catalog.

- It's not a big party school.

- It's really technical.

- The workload is almost overwhelming.

- Learning to manage your time is crucial.

- It's not a good school for people who are undecided about their majors.

Tips to Succeed at Carnegie Mellon

- Pick classes you actually like.

- Research your professors before choosing your classes.

- Actually go to class.

- Don't ever fall behind.

- Check your e-mail at least ten times a day.

- Do your homework yourself so you actually understand the material.

- Ask the TAs tons of questions.

- Always dispute bad grades.

- Know what you want to study before coming here.

Carnegie Mellon Urban Legends

- Bill Gates once offered to hire CMU's whole graduating Computer Science class.

- *Playboy* ranked CMU the second-ugliest campus in America.

- Endowment at CMU is very small, which is supposedly why its ranking doesn't go up.

- Wean Hall houses back-up computers for the Department of Defense.

- A complete network of steam tunnels provides an underground way to get around the whole campus.

School Spirit

Even if students aren't bursting with school spirit, they're still proud of the Carnegie Mellon name. Because there's an overwhelming lack of popular sports teams and the colleges within the University are fairly segregated, students don't have much to unite and rally around. Engineers, drama students, business majors, and arc-ies (Architecture) all swell with pride for their fields of study. It's not uncommon to see students wearing clothing that bears the CMU logo, but it's rare that students will dress up beyond that. During the popular Carnival Week, when students are racing in buggies and building booths, school spirit is at a yearly high. A fair share of the on-campus population will even express a subdued hatred for the University because of all the work they have to do.

Carnegie Mellon Traditions

Bagpipes
CMU has a strange and storied tradition of bagpipe-playing. It's not uncommon to hear the comforting (shrill) noise of the pipes floating through campus on almost any night of the week. This is one of CMU's more eccentric, endearing traditions that has come to grow on students. CMU is the only university in the country to offer a degree in bagpipe music.

Buggy
Buggies are small, cylindrical push carts that students race around the campus streets during Carnival Week. The buggies are piloted by a "pusher" and are steered by the driver, a female student who is situated within the buggy. Students prepare all year, building and testing their buggies so that they'll be ready to race in time for Spring Carnival.

Clippership
The Clippership is constantly offering leisure boat trips around Pittsburgh's three rivers. During orientation week, CMU reserves an entire ship for the incoming freshmen class to party on all night. Upon graduation, seniors ride the ship again in a trip bidding farewell to CMU. As a freshman, it's a great way to meet new friends. As a senior, it's a fun way to say goodbye to everyone you've gotten to know over your CMU career.

Dancers' Symposium
Dancers' Symposium is held yearly at the end of Fall and Spring semester. The show features student-choreographed dances ranging in style from ballet to hip-hop. Any student can volunteer to dance or choreograph a dance. Many students perform in more than one dance.

The Fence
In the middle of he Cut, at the center of CMU's campus, is the Fence. While the Fence itself serves no practical purpose, it's a Carnegie Mellon tradition for students to paint personal messages or advertisements for parties on it. Students can only paint the Fence after midnight, and once it's painted, they must sleep outside to guard it from other students eager to paint it again before sunrise.

Greek Sing

Greek Sing is an annual event where CMU's Greek organizations perform original song and dance routines to support a local charitable organization. Every March, the fraternities and sororities compete to raise money for a good cause and to see which Greek organizations can put on the best show.

The Green Room Wall

A tradition within the College of Fine Arts is for senior drama students to autograph the Green Room's walls and ceilings before graduating. The Green Room is located on campus behind the stage of Kresge Theatre.

The Kiltie Band

Decked out in full Scottish gear and ready to release blaring bagpipe music, CMU's Kiltie Band an 80-plus year tradition is an antiquated but beloved campus tradition. The band has been performing at every home football game since CMU hosted Notre Dame on Andrew Carnegie's birthday in 1922.

Finding a Job or Internship

The Lowdown On...
Finding a Job or Internship

If you are worried about finding a job after going to school, don't feel like you're on your own. The CMU Career Center offers a number of services for its students. Just keep in mind that many students still cite networking as one of the best ways to make connections and find a job.

Advice

From the moment you walk on campus, get in touch and stay in contact with the Career Center. Also, the BOC (Business Opportunities Conference), TOC (Technical Opportunities Conference), and TIE (Technical Internship Exposition) are crucial conferences to attend.

Career Center Resources & Services

Campus Employment

Career Counseling

Placement Advising

Career Workshops

The Resource Center

Graduate School Advising

TartanTRAK

Career Center Announcement B-Board
cmu.career-center.announce (upcoming events, campus interview postings, job fair announcements)

Average Salary Information

The Lowdown

The following statistics represent average starting salaries for CMU graduates by major, current as of 2005. If the information for a specific major does not exist, it means that fewer than four students have reported salary offers.

Carnegie Institute of Technology

Chemical Engineering	$58,000
Civil & Environmental Engineering	$46,800
Electrical & Computer Engineering	$57,000
Material Sciences & Engineering	$52,200
Mechanical Engineering	$52,100

College of Fine Arts

Information Not Available

Mellon College of Science

Biology	$39,960
Chemistry	$52,620
Mathematics	$53,791
Physics	$55,314
Social & Decision Sciences	$43,000

Humanities and Social Sciences

Economics	$42,142
English	$44,498
Psychology	$36,900
Information Systems	$55,727

Tepper School of Business

Computing & Information Technology	$55,000
Finance	$53,650
General Management	$53,100
Manufacturing, Management & Consulting	$53,800
Marketing	$46,900
Overall	$55,200

School of Computer Science

Computer Science	$63,000

Graduates Who Enter Job Market Within

6 Months: 60%

1 Year: 80%

2 Years: 95%

Firms That Most Frequently Hire Graduates

Accenture, American Management Systems, Bank of America, Boeing, Ford Motor Company, Harris, IBM, Intel, Lehman Brothers, Lockheed Martin, Merck, Microsoft, Oracle, PPG, Westinghouse

Alumni

The Lowdown On...
Alumni

Web Site:
www.cmu.edu/alumni

E-mail:
Alumni-house@andrew.cmu.
edu

Services Available:
Lifetime e-mail forwarding

Office:
Alumni House
5017 Forbes Ave
Pittsburgh, PA 15213
(800) 2-CMU-ALUM

The Alumni House

The Alumni House is right across the street from the UC and has meeting rooms, a small kitchen, and a friendly staff. It is open 8:30 a.m.–5 p.m. on weekdays during the regular school year. The office of alumni relations supports the 60,000 member Carnegie Mellon Alumni Association.

Major Alumni Events

The biggest events for alumni are Homecoming, Spring Carnival, and Class Reunions. Homecoming takes place in October and features a football game; Spring Carnival is in April and features buggy and booth; and class reunions take place year-round and can be found on the alumni Web site.

Alumni Publications

Carnegie Mellon Magazine

Carnegie Mellon Magazine comes out four times a year and engages 81,000 readers to keep them up-to-speed with CMU life. Yearly subscriptions are $8.

Did You Know?

Famous CMU Alums

Ted Danson (Class of '72), star of TV Show *Cheers*

Holly Hunter (Class of '80), star of movie *The Piano*

Vinod Khosla (Class of '78), former CEO of Sun Microsystems and leading Silicon Valley venture capitalist

Rob Marshall (Class of '82), Academy Award winning director/choreographer

Andy Warhol (Class of '49), founded the '60s pop art movement, died in 1987

John Wells (Class of '66), creator and producer of TV Shows *Hill Street Blues*, *LA Law*, and *NYPD Blue*

Ming-Na Wen (Class of '86), voice of Mulan and actress in the *Joy Luck Club* and *ER*

Student Organizations

Activities Board - *www.andrew.cmu.edu/org/AB*

Aikido - *www.andrew.cmu.edu/org/aikido*

ALLIES - An organization for people of all sexual orientations coming together to support gays, lesbians, and bisexuals. *www.andrew.cmu.edu/allies*

Amnesty International - Carnegie Mellon Chapter *www.andrew.cmu.edu/org/amnesty-int*

Asian Student Association (ASA)

Association for India's Development (AID) - *www.andrew.cmu.edu/~aid*

Association for Industrial Management and Economics (AIME)- *www.andrew.cmu.edu/~aime*

Astronomy Club - *www.contrib.andrew.cmu.edu/~astroc*

Bagpipe Band - *www.andrew.cmu.edu/~pipeband*

Ballroom Dance Club - *www.contrib.andrew.cmu.edu/ ~ballroom*

Black Graduate Student Organization (BGSO) - *www.andrew.cmu.edu/org/BGSO*

Bridge Club - *www.andrew.cmu.edu/~dr4b/bridge-club.html*

Carnegie Threads - Quilting Club *www.contrib.andrew.cmu.edu/~quilt/home.html*

Christians on Campus

CMU College Republicans - *www.andrew.cmu.edu/~cmucr*

CMU Masters Swimming Club

cmuOUT - A group of lesbian, gay, and bisexual members of the campus community, and their friends. *www.andrew.cmu.edu/~out*

Cycling Club - *www.andrew.cmu.edu/~cycling*

Dancer's Symposium - *www.andrew.cmu.edu/org/dancer/ DANCERSYMPOSIUM.html*

Doctors of Carnegie

Earth - CMU's environmental club *www.andrew.cmu.edu/org/earth*

East End Tutoring Program - *outreach.mac.cc.cmu.edu/EEYP/EastEnd.html*

Eclectic Studies Group - *www.contrib.andrew.cmu.edu/~eclectic*

Emergency Medical Service (CMU EMS) - *www.andrew.cmu. edu/~cmu/ems*

Eta Kappa Nu - The International Honor Society for Electrical Engineers. *www.ece.cmu.edu/~hkn*

Explorers Club - An outdoor activities club. *www.andrew.cmu.edu/org/explorers*

Fiesta – Organizes a campus-wide celebration, in honor of the past academic year and in anticipation of summer. *www.andrew.cmu.edu/~fiesta*

Filmmaking@cmu - *www.andrew.cmu.edu/proj/film*

Fringe - Promotes a spirit of friendship.

Hong Kong Students' - Association - *www.andrew.cmu.edu/org/hksa*

Ice Hockey Club - *www.andrew.cmu.edu/user/hockey/index.html*

Joyful Noise - A Christian a cappella singing group. *www.andrew.cmu.edu/~jn*

KGB *www.contrib.andrew.cmu.edu/org/kgb*

Mayur - An Indian Student Organization. *www.contrib.andrew.cmu.edu/~mm3m*

Muslim Students Association of CMU - *www.andrew.cmu.edu/~msa*

Oakland Review - Carnegie Mellon University's annual literary-arts journal. *english.cmu.edu/or*

CMU Origami Club - *www.contrib.andrew.cmu.edu/org/origami/home.html*

Pi Delta Psi Fraternity, Inc.

Persian Student Organization (PSO)

PIONEERS - *www.andrew.cmu.edu/user/pioneers*

SALSA - A Latin and Hispanic culture club.

Scotch'n'Soda Theater - Carnegie Mellon's student-run *theater company. www.andrew.cmu.edu/~sns*

Society of Hispanic Professional Engineers (SHPE)

Society of Physics Students

Society of Women Engineers - *www.andrew.cmu.edu/org/swe*

SPIC MACAY - Society for the Promotion of Indian Classical Music and Culture Amongst Youth.

Carnegie Mellon Speech & Parliamentary Debate Society *www.andrew.cmu.edu/org/debate*

Spring Carnival - *www.andrew.cmu.edu/org/carnival*

String Ensemble

Students for the Exploration and Development of Space - Only international space organization run entirely by students.

Student Pugwash

Student Senate - *www.andrew.cmu.edu/user/ss2p*

Student Union - Carnegie Mellon's alternative news journal.

Taiwanese Students Association - *www.andrew.cmu.edu/~tsa*

Tau Beta Pi, Pennsylvania Gamma chapter

WRCT 88.3 fm - Carnegie Mellon's student-run radio station. *www.wrct.org*

The Best & Worst

The Ten BEST Things About Carnegie Mellon University

1	Carnival
2	Diversity
3	Plays at the Purnell Center
4	Painting the Fence at midnight
5	The $1 movies in the UC
6	Flirting through e-mail & Instant Messenger
7	Chillin' on the Cut on a nice day
8	PHI on Thursday nights
9	Restaurants with late-night, half-price food
10	Bagpipes

The Ten **WORST** Things About Carnegie Mellon University

1 Bagpipes

2 Finding a parking spot

3 Meal plan/dining

4 Sporadic weather

5 The Hub

6 Teachers with heavy accents

7 The Smell of the Old Student Center

8 Skibo Gym

9 Introverts

10 Boy/girl ratio

Visiting

The Lowdown On...
Visiting

Hotel Information:

Shadyside

Appletree Bed and Breakfast
www.appletreeb-b.com
703 S. Negley Ave.
Pittsburgh, PA 15232
(412) 661-0631
Distance from Campus:
Less than a mile
Price Range: $140–$190

Friendship Suites
www.friendshipsuites.com
301 Stratford Ave.
Pittsburgh, PA 15232
(412) 392-1935
Distance from Campus:
1.5 miles
Price Range: $79–$119

➜

Shadyside Inn

www.shadysideinn.com
5405 Fifth Ave.
Pittsburgh, PA 15232
(412) 682-2300
Distance from Campus:
Less than a mile
Price Range: $99–$139

Sunnyledge

5124 Fifth Ave.
Pittsburgh, PA 15232
(412) 683-5014
Distance from Campus:
Less than a mile
Price Range: $139–$275

Oakland

Best Western - University Center

www.bestwestern.com
3401 Boulevard of the Allies
Pittsburgh, PA 15213
(412) 683-6100
(800) 245-4444
Distance from Campus:
1.4 miles
Price Range: $85

Hampton Inn

*www.pittsburghhamptoninn
.com*
3315 Hamlet St.
Pittsburgh, PA 15213
(412) 681-1000
(800) HAMPTON

(Hampton Inn, continued)

Distance from Campus:
1.4 miles
Price Range: $89–$119

Holiday Inn Select - University Center

*www.basshotels.com
/holiday-inn*
100 Lytton Ave.
Pittsburgh, PA 15213
(412) 682-6200
(800) 864-8287
Distance from Campus:
Less than a mile
Price Range: $123–$144

Residence Inn by Marriott

www.residenceinn.com
3896 Bigelow Blvd.
Pittsburgh, PA 15213
(412) 621-2200
(800) 331-3131
Distance from Campus:
1 mile
Price Range: $139–$189

University Club

123 University Pl.
Pittsburgh, PA 15213
(412) 621-1890
Distance from Campus:
Less than 1 mile
Price Range: $99–$109

Wyndham Garden Hotel – University Place

www.wyndham.com
3454 Forbes Ave.
Pittsburgh, PA 15213
(412) 683-2040
(877) 662-6242
Distance from Campus:
1 mile
Price Range: $89–$129

Downtown

Hilton Towers

www.hilton.com
600 Commonwealth Pl.
Pittsburgh, PA 15222
(412) 391-4600
Distance from Campus:
4.2 miles
Price Range: $189–$219

Morning Glory Inn Bed and Breakfast

*www.morningglorybedand
breakfast.com*
2119 Sarah St.
Pittsburgh, PA 15203
(412) 431-1707
Distance from Campus:
3 miles
Price Range: $150–$190

Omni William Penn

www.omnihotels.com
530 William Penn Pl.
Pittsburgh, PA 15219
(412) 281-7100

(Omni William Penn, continued)

Distance from Campus:
4 miles
Price Range: $116–$159

Pittsburgh Marriott City Center

www.marriott.com/pitdt
112 Washington Pl.
Pittsburgh, PA 15219
412-471-4000
(888) 456-6600
Distance from Campus:
5 miles
Price Range: $99–$159

Renaissance Pittsburgh Hotel

*www.renaissancehotels.
com*
107 Sixth St.
Pittsburgh, PA 15222
412-562-1200
(866) 454-4400
Distance from Campus:
3 miles
Price Range: $129–$169

Sheraton Hotel-Station Square

www.sheraton.com
7 Station Square Dr.
Pittsburgh, PA 15219
(412) 261-2000
(800) 255-7488
Distance from Campus:
4.2 miles
Price Range: $79–$119

→

Westin Convention Center Pittsburgh

www.westin.com/pittsburgh

1000 Penn Ave.

Pittsburgh, PA 15222

(412) 281-3700

(800) 367-8478

Distance from Campus:
4 miles

Price Range: $89–$225

Take a Campus Virtual Tour

www.cmu.edu/vrtour

Campus Tours

Campus tours run most Mondays through Fridays (except on holidays, between semesters, during finals and during spring break). Tours depart at 9:30 a.m., 11:30 a.m., 1:30 p.m., and 3:30 p.m. Call in advance of your visit to check the availability of the tour!

To Schedule a Group Information Session or Interview

Call (412) 268-2082 on any weekday from 8:30 a.m.–5 p.m. Eastern Standard Time.

The admission staff interviews most Mondays through Fridays throughout the year; however, because of the time involved in reviewing applications, no interviews will be conducted from January 1 through May 1.

Sleeping Bag Weekend

Wanna live the life of a CMU student for a day and a half? Try visiting CMU during a Sleeping Bag Weekend. Expect to receive an invitation from CMU if you are on their mailing list. If you are not on their mailing list, call (412) 268-2082 or e-mail cmsbw@andrew.cmu.edu. During Sleeping Bag Weekend, you'll be able to meet other CMU students, faculty, deans, and admissions officers, so bring this book with you and grill everyone you can with questions!

Important Tip!

Remember, Sleeping Bag Weekend might be the greatest time of your life, but even one and a half days at CMU might not give you an accurate portrayal of campus.

Prowl Around!

Go find some students at the UC that are just hanging out. Most students at CMU can be very helpful if you take the initiative to introduce yourself and nicely ask them for help.

Directions to Campus

Driving from the North/West

- Take the Pennsylvania Turnpike east to Exit 28, Perry Highway

- Follow Interstate 79 South to 279 South (Exit 72)

- Follow signs and go over the Fort Duquesne Bridge

- Take 376 East to Exit 2A, Forbes Avenue/Oakland

- Stay in the right-hand lanes, following Forbes 1.3 miles through the Oakland business district to campus

- Turn right into the parking garage on campus

Driving from the South

- Take Interstate 79 North to 279 North (Pittsburgh)

- Follow 279 North toward Pittsburgh through the Fort Pitt Tunnel and onto the Fort Pitt Bridge

- Once on the bridge, stay in the far right lanes and follow signs for 376 East/Monroeville

- Take 376 East to Exit 2A, Forbes Avenue/Oakland

- Stay in the right-hand lanes, following Forbes 1.3 miles through the Oakland business district to campus

- Turn right into the parking garage on campus

Driving from the East

- Take the Pennsylvania Turnpike West to Exit 57, Pittsburgh/Monroeville

- Follow Interstate 376 West to Exit 7, Edgewood/Swissvale

- Turn right onto Braddock Avenue (at the end of the ramp)

- Continue to the Forbes Avenue inter-section (Frick Park will be on the left)

- Turn left onto Forbes Avenue and follow Forbes Avenue approximately three miles to campus

- Turn left into the parking garage on campus

Words to Know

Academic Probation – A suspension imposed on a student if he or she fails to keep up with the school's minimum academic requirements. Those unable to improve their grades after receiving this warning can face dismissal.

Beer Pong/Beirut – A drinking game involving cups of beer arranged in a pyramid shape on each side of a table. The goal is to get a ping pong ball into one of the opponent's cups by throwing the ball or hitting it with a paddle. If the ball lands in a cup, the opponent is required to drink the beer.

Bid – An invitation from a fraternity or sorority to 'pledge' (join) that specific house.

Blue-Light Phone – Brightly-colored phone posts with a blue light bulb on top. These phones exist for security purposes and are located at various outside locations around most campuses. In an emergency, a student can pick up one of these phones (free of charge) to connect with campus police or a security escort.

Campus Police – Police who are specifically assigned to a given institution. Campus police are typically not regular city officers; they are employed by the university in a full-time capacity.

Club Sports – A level of sports that falls somewhere between varsity and intramural. If a student is unable to commit to a varsity team but has a lot of passion for athletics, a club sport could be a better, less intense option. Even less demanding, intramural (IM) sports often involve no traveling and considerably less time.

Cocaine – An illegal drug. Also known as "coke" or "blow," cocaine often resembles a white crystalline or powdery substance. It is highly addictive and dangerous.

Common Application – An application with which students can apply to multiple schools.

Course Registration – The period of official class selection for the upcoming quarter or semester. Prior to registration, it is best to prepare several back-up courses in case a particular class becomes full. If a course is full, students can place themselves on the waitlist, although this still does not guarantee entry.

Division Athletics – Athletic classifications range from Division I to Division III. Division IA is the most competitive, while Division III is considered to be the least competitive.

Dorm – A dorm (or dormitory) is an on-campus housing facility. Dorms can provide a range of options from suite-style rooms to more communal options that include shared bathrooms. Most first-year students live in dorms. Some upperclassmen who wish to stay on campus also choose this option.

Early Action – An application option with which a student can apply to a school and receive an early acceptance response without a binding commitment. This system is becoming less and less available.

Early Decision – An application option that students should use only if they are certain they plan to attend the school in question. If a student applies using the early decision option and is admitted, he or she is required and bound to attend that university. Admission rates are usually higher among students who apply through early decision, as the student is clearly indicating that the school is his or her first choice.

Ecstasy – An illegal drug. Also known as "E" or "X," ecstasy looks like a pill and most resembles an aspirin. Considered a party drug, ecstasy is very dangerous and can be deadly.

Ethernet – An extremely fast Internet connection available in most university-owned residence halls. To use an Ethernet connection properly, a student will need a network card and cable for his or her computer.

Fake ID – A counterfeit identification card that contains false information. Most commonly, students get fake IDs with altered birthdates so that they appear to be older than 21 (and therefore of legal drinking age). Even though it is illegal, many college students have fake IDs in hopes of purchasing alcohol or getting into bars.

Frosh – Slang for "freshman" or "freshmen."

Hazing – Initiation rituals administered by some fraternities or sororities as part of the pledging process. Many universities have outlawed hazing due to its degrading, and sometimes dangerous, nature.

Intramurals (IMs) – A popular, and usually free, sport league in which students create teams and compete against one another. These sports vary in competitiveness and can include a range of activities—everything from billiards to water polo. IM sports are a great way to meet people with similar interests.

Keg – Officially called a half-barrel, a keg contains roughly 200 12-ounce servings of beer.

LSD – An illegal drug, also known as acid, this hallucinogenic drug most commonly resembles a tab of paper.

Marijuana – An illegal drug, also known as weed or pot; along with alcohol, marijuana is one of the most commonly-found drugs on campuses across the country.

Major –The focal point of a student's college studies; a specific topic that is studied for a degree. Examples of majors include physics, English, history, computer science, economics, business, and music. Many students decide on a specific major before arriving on campus, while others are simply "undecided" until declaring a major. Those who are extremely interested in two areas can also choose to double major.

Meal Block – The equivalent of one meal. Students on a meal plan usually receive a fixed number of meals per week. Each meal, or "block," can be redeemed at the school's dining facilities in place of cash. Often, a student's weekly allotment of meal blocks will be forfeited if not used.

Minor – An additional focal point in a student's education. Often serving as a complement or addition to a student's main area of focus, a minor has fewer requirements and prerequisites to fulfill than a major. Minors are not required for graduation from most schools; however some students who want to explore many different interests choose to pursue both a major and a minor.

Mushrooms – An illegal drug. Also known as "'shrooms," this drug resembles regular mushrooms but is extremely hallucinogenic.

Off-Campus Housing – Housing from a particular landlord or rental group that is not affiliated with the university. Depending on the college, off-campus housing can range from extremely popular to non-existent. Students who choose to live off campus are typically given more freedom, but they also have to deal with possible subletting scenarios, furniture, bills, and other issues. In addition to these factors, rental prices and distance often affect a student's decision to move off campus.

Office Hours – Time that teachers set aside for students who have questions about coursework. Office hours are a good forum for students to go over any problems and to show interest in the subject material.

Pledging – The early phase of joining a fraternity or sorority, pledging takes place after a student has gone through rush and received a bid. Pledging usually lasts between one and two semesters. Once the pledging period is complete and a particular student has done everything that is required to become a member, that student is considered a brother or sister. If a fraternity or a sorority would decide to "haze" a group of students, this initiation would take place during the pledging period.

Private Institution – A school that does not use tax revenue to subsidize education costs. Private schools typically cost more than public schools and are usually smaller.

Prof – Slang for "professor."

Public Institution – A school that uses tax revenue to subsidize education costs. Public schools are often a good value for in-state residents and tend to be larger than most private colleges.

Quarter System (or Trimester System) – A type of academic calendar system. In this setup, students take classes for three academic periods. The first quarter usually starts in late September or early October and concludes right before Christmas. The second quarter usually starts around early to mid–January and finishes up around March or April. The last academic quarter, or "third quarter," usually starts in late March or early April and finishes up in late May or Mid-June. The fourth quarter is summer. The major difference between the quarter system and semester system is that students take more, less comprehensive courses under the quarter calendar.

RA (Resident Assistant) – A student leader who is assigned to a particular floor in a dormitory in order to help to the other students who live there. An RA's duties include ensuring student safety and providing assistance wherever possible.

Recitation – An extension of a specific course; a review session. Some classes, particularly large lectures, are supplemented with mandatory recitation sessions that provide a relatively personal class setting.

Rolling Admissions – A form of admissions. Most commonly found at public institutions, schools with this type of policy continue to accept students throughout the year until their class sizes are met. For example, some schools begin accepting students as early as December and will continue to do so until April or May.

Room and Board – This figure is typically the combined cost of a university-owned room and a meal plan.

Room Draw/Housing Lottery – A common way to pick on-campus room assignments for the following year. If a student decides to remain in university-owned housing, he or she is assigned a unique number that, along with seniority, is used to determine his or her housing for the next year.

Rush – The period in which students can meet the brothers and sisters of a particular chapter and find out if a given fraternity or sorority is right for them. Rushing a fraternity or a sorority is not a requirement at any school. The goal of rush is to give students who are serious about pledging a feel for what to expect.

Semester System – The most common type of academic calendar system at college campuses. This setup typically includes two semesters in a given school year. The fall semester starts around the end of August or early September and concludes before winter vacation. The spring semester usually starts in mid-January and ends in late April or May.

Student Center/Rec Center/Student Union – A common area on campus that often contains study areas, recreation facilities, and eateries. This building is often a good place to meet up with fellow students; depending on the school, the student center can have a huge role or a non-existent role in campus life.

Student ID – A university-issued photo ID that serves as a student's key to school-related functions. Some schools require students to show these cards in order to get into dorms, libraries, cafeterias, and other facilities. In addition to storing meal plan information, in some cases, a student ID can actually work as a debit card and allow students to purchase things from bookstores or local shops.

Suite – A type of dorm room. Unlike dorms that feature communal bathrooms shared by the entire floor, suites offer bathrooms shared only among the suite. Suite-style dorm rooms can house anywhere from two to ten students.

TA (Teacher's Assistant) – An undergraduate or grad student who helps in some manner with a specific course. In some cases, a TA will teach a class, assist a professor, grade assignments, or conduct office hours.

Undergraduate – A student in the process of studying for his or her bachelor's degree.

ABOUT THE AUTHOR

I had a great time writing this book! I've been looking for a chance to express myself through my writing, and the entire experience has been very exciting. I'm hoping to publish more in the future as I continue to grow as a writer. I'm tirelessly pursuing degrees in both professional writing and business administration at Carnegie Mellon. In the future, I hope to utilize the skills I've learned in both of my majors. Pittsburgh is the first place I've lived since leaving my native Northern New Jersey. Coming to college here has been a dizzying and maturing experience to say the least. I hope this book has been insightful for you, and I hope you had a few laughs while reading it. If you have any questions or comments please contact me by e-mail.

Here's where my biography takes a turn from overly narcissistic self commentary. I'd like to give many people many thanks. Thank you Mom, Dad, Amanda, Grandpa, Ragonesis, Kobuskies, Liebermann's, Becky, CheeChee, Tom, Aaron, Drew, Jeremy, Meredith, Red Beavis, Rose, Mr. Gaul, Horatio Flatbush, Honus, Jason, Jen, Johnson, Keara, Nick, Scott, and everyone at College Prowler!

Daniel Liebermann
danielliebermann@collegeprowler.com

California Colleges

California dreamin'?

This book is a must have for you!

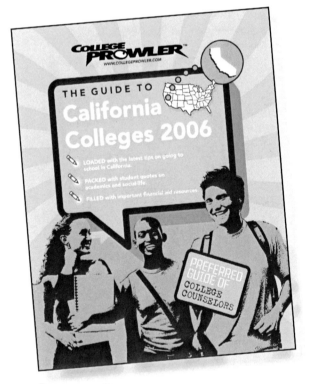

CALIFORNIA COLLEGES
7¼" X 10", 762 Pages Paperback
$29.95 Retail
1-59658-501-3

Stanford, UC Berkeley, Caltech—California is home to some of America's greatest institutes of higher learning. *California Colleges* gives the lowdown on 24 of the best, side by side, in one prodigious volume.

New England Colleges

Looking for peace in the Northeast?
Pick up this regional guide to New England!

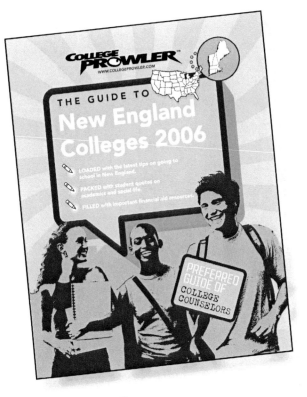

NEW ENGLAND COLLEGES
7¼" X 10", 1015 Pages Paperback
$29.95 Retail
1-59658-504-8

New England is the birthplace of many prestigious universities, and with so many to choose from, picking the right school can be a tough decision. With inside information on over 34 competive Northeastern schools, *New England Colleges* provides the same high-quality information prospective students expect from College Prowler in one all-inclusive, easy-to-use reference.

Schools of the South

Headin' down south? This book will help you find your way to the perfect school!

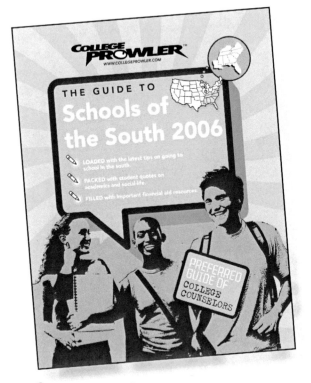

SCHOOLS OF THE SOUTH
7¼" X 10", 773 Pages Paperback
$29.95 Retail
1-59658-503-X

Southern pride is always strong. Whether it's across town or across state, many Southern students are devoted to their home sweet home. *Schools of the South* offers an honest student perspective on 36 universities available south of the Mason-Dixon.

Untangling
the Ivy League

The ultimate book for everything Ivy!

UNTANGLING THE IVY LEAGUE
7¼" X 10", 567 Pages Paperback
$24.95 Retail
1-59658-500-5

Ivy League students, alumni, admissions officers, and other top insiders get together to tell it like it is. *Untangling the Ivy League* covers every aspect—from admissions and athletics to secret societies and urban legends—of the nation's eight oldest, wealthiest, and most competitive colleges and universities.

Need Help Paying For School?

Apply for our scholarship!

College Prowler awards thousands of dollars a year to students who compose the best essays. E-mail scholarship@collegeprowler.com for more information, or call 1-800-290-2682.

Apply now at ***www.collegeprowler.com***

Tell Us What Life Is Really Like at Your School!

Have you ever wanted to let people know what your college is really like? Now's your chance to help millions of high school students choose the right college.

Let your voice be heard.

Check out ***www.collegeprowler.com*** for more info!

Need More Help?

Do you have more questions about this school? Can't find a certain statistic? College Prowler is here to help. We are the best source of college information out there. We have a network of thousands of students who can get the latest information on any school to you ASAP. E-mail us at info@collegeprowler.com with your college-related questions.

E-Mail Us Your College-Related Questions!

Check out *www.collegeprowler.com* for more details.
1-800-290-2682

Write For Us!

Get published! Voice your opinion.

Writing a College Prowler guidebook is both fun and rewarding; our open-ended format allows your own creativity free reign. Our writers have been featured in national newspapers and have seen their names in bookstores across the country. Now is your chance to break into the publishing industry with one of the country's fastest-growing publishers!

Apply now at ***www.collegeprowler.com***

Contact editor@collegeprowler.com or call 1-800-290-2682 for more details.

Pros and Cons

Still can't figure out if this is the right school for you?
You've already read through this in-depth guide; why not
list the pros and cons? It will really help with narrowing down
your decision and determining whether or not
this school is right for you.

Pros

....

....

....

....

....

....

....

....

....

....

....

....

Cons

....

....

....

....

....

....

....

....

....

....

....

....

Pros and Cons

Still can't figure out if this is the right school for you?
You've already read through this in-depth guide; why not
list the pros and cons? It will really help with narrowing down
your decision and determining whether or not
this school is right for you.

Pros

....

....

....

....

....

....

....

....

....

....

....

....

Cons

....

....

....

....

....

....

....

....

....

....

....

....

Notes

Order now! • collegeprowler.com • 1.800.290.2682
Over 260 single-school guidebooks!

Albion College
Alfred University
Allegheny College
American University
Amherst College
Arizona State University
Auburn University
Babson College
Ball State University
Bard College
Barnard College
Bates College
Baylor University
Beloit College
Bentley College
Binghamton University
Birmingham Southern College
Boston College
Boston University
Bowdoin College
Brandeis University
Brigham Young University
Brown University
Bryn Mawr College
Bucknell University
Cal Poly
Cal Poly Pomona
Cal State Northridge
Cal State Sacramento
Caltech
Carleton College
Carnegie Mellon University
Case Western Reserve
Centenary College of Louisiana
Centre College
Claremont McKenna College
Clark Atlanta University
Clark University
Clemson University
Colby College
Colgate University
College of Charleston
College of the Holy Cross
College of William & Mary
College of Wooster
Colorado College
Columbia University
Connecticut College
Cornell University
Creighton University
CUNY Hunters College
Dartmouth College
Davidson College
Denison University
DePauw University
Dickinson College
Drexel University
Duke University
Duquesne University
Earlham College
East Carolina University
Elon University
Emerson College
Emory University
FIT
Florida State University
Fordham University

Franklin & Marshall College
Furman University
Geneva College
George Washington University
Georgetown University
Georgia Tech
Gettysburg College
Gonzaga University
Goucher College
Grinnell College
Grove City College
Guilford College
Gustavus Adolphus College
Hamilton College
Hampshire College
Hampton University
Hanover College
Harvard University
Harvey Mudd College
Haverford College
Hofstra University
Hollins University
Howard University
Idaho State University
Illinois State University
Illinois Wesleyan University
Indiana University
Iowa State University
Ithaca College
IUPUI
James Madison University
Johns Hopkins University
Juniata College
Kansas State
Kent State University
Kenyon College
Lafayette College
LaRoche College
Lawrence University
Lehigh University
Lewis & Clark College
Louisiana State University
Loyola College in Maryland
Loyola Marymount University
Loyola University Chicago
Loyola University New Orleans
Macalester College
Marlboro College
Marquette University
McGill University
Miami University of Ohio
Michigan State University
Middle Tennessee State
Middlebury College
Millsaps College
MIT
Montana State University
Mount Holyoke College
Muhlenberg College
New York University
North Carolina State
Northeastern University
Northern Arizona University
Northern Illinois University
Northwestern University
Oberlin College
Occidental College

Ohio State University
Ohio University
Ohio Wesleyan University
Old Dominion University
Penn State University
Pepperdine University
Pitzer College
Pomona College
Princeton University
Providence College
Purdue University
Reed College
Rensselaer Polytechnic Institute
Rhode Island School of Design
Rhodes College
Rice University
Rochester Institute of Technology
Rollins College
Rutgers University
San Diego State University
Santa Clara University
Sarah Lawrence College
Scripps College
Seattle University
Seton Hall University
Simmons College
Skidmore College
Slippery Rock
Smith College
Southern Methodist University
Southwestern University
Spelman College
St. Joseph's University Philladelphia
St. John's University
St. Louis University
St. Olaf College
Stanford University
Stetson University
Stony Brook University
Susquehanna University
Swarthmore College
Syracuse University
Temple University
Tennessee State University
Texas A & M University
Texas Christian University
Towson University
Trinity College Connecticut
Trinity University Texas
Truman State
Tufts University
Tulane University
UC Berkeley
UC Davis
UC Irvine
UC Riverside
UC San Diego
UC Santa Barbara
UC Santa Cruz
UCLA
Union College
University at Albany
University at Buffalo
University of Alabama
University of Arizona
University of Central Florida
University of Chicago

University of Colorado
University of Connecticut
University of Delaware
University of Denver
University of Florida
University of Georgia
University of Illinois
University of Iowa
University of Kansas
University of Kentucky
University of Maine
University of Maryland
University of Massachusetts
University of Miami
University of Michigan
University of Minnesota
University of Mississippi
University of Missouri
University of Nebraska
University of New Hampshire
University of North Carolina
University of Notre Dame
University of Oklahoma
University of Oregon
University of Pennsylvania
University of Pittsburgh
University of Puget Sound
University of Rhode Island
University of Richmond
University of Rochester
University of San Diego
University of San Francisco
University of South Carolina
University of South Dakota
University of South Florida
University of Southern California
University of Tennessee
University of Texas
University of Utah
University of Vermont
University of Virginia
University of Washington
University of Wisconsin
UNLV
Ursinus College
Valparaiso University
Vanderbilt University
Vassar College
Villanova University
Virginia Tech
Wake Forest University
Warren Wilson College
Washington and Lee University
Washington University in St. Louis
Wellesley College
Wesleyan University
West Point
West Virginia University
Wheaton College IL
Wheaton College MA
Whitman College
Wilkes University
Williams College
Xavier University
Yale University

Notes

....

....

....

....

....

....

....

....

....

....

....

....

....